KEEP 'ER LIT

Keep 'Er Lit
New Selected Lyrics

VAN MORRISON

edited by EAMONN HUGHES
foreword by PAUL MULDOON

FABER & FABER

First published in the UK and the USA in 2020
by Faber & Faber Ltd
Bloomsbury House
74–77 Great Russell Street
London WC1B 3DA

Typeset by Faber & Faber Ltd
Printed in Germany by GGP Media GmbH, Pößneck

A CIP record for this book
is available from the British Library

ISBN 978–0–571–35389–7
LIMITED EDITION ISBN 978–0–571–35390–3
DELUXE EDITION ISBN 978–0–571–35391–0

10 9 8 7 6 5 4 3 2 1

Contents

Dweller on the Threshold *by Paul Muldoon*

The great artist is not only on the front line but engaged in single combat. The opponent is a version of himself and, almost inevitably, it's a fight to the death.

At the champion's back is a wall of spearmen, cheering and jeering him on. Each of them bears a wound from him and has, in turn, given him a wound. It's often a spear-thrust to the heart, a spear-thrust all have somehow survived.

Some of the spearmen at Van Morrison's back were conscripted by his father, George, who had spent time in Detroit in the early 1950s and accumulated a substantial record collection from Solly Lipsitz's record shop (Atlantic Records) in Belfast's Smithfield market. Muddy Waters, Charlie Parker, Mahalia Jackson, Woody Guthrie, Hank Williams, Sonny Terry and Brownie McGhee, John Lee Hooker, Lead Belly. Like many great artists, Van Morrison seems to lend credibility to the notion of the '10,000 hours' of limbering up they put in before reaching their full potential and coming into their own. It's a phenomenon made popular by Malcolm Gladwell in *Outliers*. In fact, I've heard Van refer to Malcolm Gladwell as he talks about serving his time, from the age of twelve, in the business of writing and performance. Between 1957 and 1964, he was involved with at least a dozen bands.

I first heard a recording of Van Morrison in 1964 when he was the lead singer of Them. I didn't know at the time the name of that band was pilfered from a *Melody Maker* ad for a group called Shorty and Them. I assumed the band name was primarily a version of the Northern Irish representation of otherness – them'uns. From the outset, Van Morrison seemed at once familiar and foreign, a straddler of traditions, skiffle and street scuffle, a Belfast boy who might have grown up on a bayou or on the Bowery or playing boogie-woogie. No wonder a 1992 recording of Van singing 'Gloria' with John Lee Hooker still seems the most natural thing in the world.

By the time I myself moved to Belfast, in 1969, Van Morrison was a bona fide solo star. His classic album, *Astral Weeks*, was simply left on the record player, like a frying pan on a hot plate, in countless student digs. I had a particular affection for 'Madame George', of course, particularly since in 1972–73 I lived in a spectacularly rundown student house at 124 Fitzroy Avenue and had the shock of recognition when a great artist stakes out his territory and, more importantly, allows the listener or reader to sublet. The detailing of Belfast life has seen Van Morrison no less to the fore than Ciaran Carson or Derek Mahon or Michael Longley, particularly when it comes to representing 'a sense of wonder':

Wee Alfie at the Castle Picture house
On the Castlereagh Road
Whistling on the corner next door where
He kept Johnny Mack Brown's horse
'O Sole Mio' by McGimsey
And the man who played the saw
Outside the City Hall
Pastie suppers down at Davy's Chipper,
Gravy Rings, Wagon Wheels,
Barmbracks, Snowballs

As Van Morrison's career developed he was able to take in Belfast no less readily than Beale Street, Irish diddley-dow-diddley no less readily than Bo Diddley. The Irishness of his work is evident from the very localised vocabulary of one of my favourites:

Goin' down to Monte Carlo about 25K from Nice

Goin' down to Monte Carlo about 25K from Nice
Got to get myself together, gotta get my head some peace

It's the blues line typified by 'Goin' Down to Monte Carlo', even more than soul or funk, that's the most common driving force in Van Morrison's music and lyrics. At the heart of the blues is the couplet, the mainstay of poetry in English from Chaucer through Dryden, Pope, Byron, Yeats and Owen to Eminem and Kendrick Lamar. It's a template that allows Van Morrison the flexibility to range over subject matter as diverse as 'the solid ground / In the County Down', the vicissitudes of the 'music business scene', the delighting in the music itself:

And it stoned me to my soul
Stoned me just like Jelly Roll

My own personal relationship with Van Morrison, which I feel obliged to acknowledge here, has developed only over recent years and is based on good-humoured banter and mutual contrariness, the very frequent 'wonderful remark' and considerable soul searching on whether there is, indeed, any fun to be had. Van Morrison continues to embody a parade of paradoxes; he is a very successful businessman who hates business, a celebrity who disavows celebrity culture, a supreme showman who is, as they say, pathologically shy. I can tell you that, when I attended his seventieth birthday party, I stayed later than he did. As to those who might be exercised by the question of 'Whatever Happened to PJ Proby?', I can also tell you I last spotted a very intact PJ at that same party.

One dominant theme in Van Morrison's work is the seamless relationship between things Celtic and the occult. In this he traces his line back through William Butler Yeats to William Blake. Indeed, some of the best of his songs sound as if they've been channelled through Yeats or Blake or Wordsworth:

The mountain air was fresh and clear
The sun was up behind the hill
It felt so good to be alive
On that morning in spring

I want to sing this song for you
I want to lift your spirits high
And in my soul I want to feel
The beauty of the days gone by

One of the things that makes an artist great is their recognition not only of the significance of their serving time in the writer's trade – as if one were a riveter, say, or a rat-catcher – but their recognition also that they are merely conduits for a force beyond themselves. In fact, it's the combination of these two seemingly contradictory positions that may be discerned in the most successful musicians and writers. This is the single greatest lesson to be learned from Lonnie Donegan and John Donne, Big Bill Broonzy and Rabbie Burns. As Van Morrison has himself put it:

I write from a different place. I do not even know what it is called or if it has a name.

It's this mix of genuine humility and hard-won hubris, of mysticism and technical mastery, that makes Van Morrison quite simply, and quite indisputably, 'The Bard of Belfast'.

Introduction *by Eamonn Hughes*

Van Morrison's status as an original is assured. In his early work with Them he led one of the great bands to emerge from the British blues boom, kickstarted the pop and rock scene in Ireland, and also wrote songs that have not just endured but entered the canon of popular music. Striking out on his own he then changed the way that music sounded by ignoring the lines along which it had been developing in favour of his own unique combination of sounds and words. Since then he has continued to move restlessly across forms and genres, rarely feeling any need to conform to prevailing fashions or values in either his words or his musics (and the plural is appropriate). Anyone looking for patterns in his work will quickly recognise that the overarching pattern is of disruption. As soon as he has established a sound or a set of concerns, he moves on to something different. In doing so he has produced songs that are simply necessary in the lives of the many people who use them to mark the significant moments – both joyful and melancholy – in their lives.

This is the second volume of Van Morrison's selected lyrics and it aims, like its predecessor, *Lit Up Inside* (2014), to provide a representative sample of his work. Just flicking through the book and noticing the different shapes of the songs gives an immediate sense of the many different ways that Morrison has approached the art of songwriting from tightly controlled early lyrics through more free-flowing songs or even spoken word pieces into what look like more conventional song structures. Taken together the two volumes give an overview of his work over some fifty years as a songwriter. The arrangement here is once again broadly chronological and the songs again cover a range of themes, topics, places, and people that manages to be both extensive and concentrated. Van Morrison has both extended the range of, for want of a better term, the popular song and equally he has established and returned to a core set of concerns and interests throughout his career.

Even a partial list of his recurrent interests is still extensive. It would have to include love songs, work songs (about both physical work and the work of being a songwriter), songs about the pains and anxieties of existence, songs of consolation, songs about various kinds of spiritual quest and the realms of the mystical, and songs which deal with healing and reconciliation both with the self and with others. Then there are the songs of memory and of childhood; songs about the natural world ('nature's bright green shady path' as it's called in 'Rave On, John Donne') and about the perspectives it can provide on time, which can exist both in various secular forms (the seasons, times of day) and *sub specie aeternitatis*. Places too receive due attention both in the naming of many actual towns and cities and in the form of semi-mythical locations. There are songs of falling leaves and evening shadows, of joyous sounds and whining boy moans; there are songs of wisdom and grace. There is also a long-standing concern with the 'the voice of the silence' ('Little Village'), and many tributes to the voices of musicians and writers who have been significant for Morrison.

This brief listing points in two directions. On the one hand it is possible to break these categories down into specifics. The love songs, for example, deal with love in all its guises: the just glimpsed, the domestically settled, the anguish of break-ups, the ways in which an earthy, secular love can slide almost imperceptibly into something more spiritual, the idea that love can provide an afternoon of joy, or a lifetime of meaning. Likewise, it's possible to find songs for every season of the year, and indeed for most times of the day. Contrariwise these various categories slide into and across each other: gardens as places in the natural world are also echoes of the primal mystical garden and are the setting for many love songs whether rapturous or melancholy, while the love being expressed can be either profane or spiritual (and sometimes both). There is here a basic opposition. On the one hand there is the desire of the observer and recorder of experience to note as clearly as possible the details of that experience, as in, for example, 'It was on a Sunday and the autumn leaves were on the ground' ('If You and I Could Be As Two'). For this songwriter the time of day, the weather, the season of the year, the location are all vital aspects of the experience – the emotion being recollected (whether tranquilly or not) is inextricably tied up with such details and the songs are faithful to them. This can be true even when the songs are elliptical, fragmented and episodic. Songs such as 'Astral Weeks' seem to arise from a sense of being overwhelmed and as a result all the recorder can do is out pick out occasional details from a welter of stimuli – 'pictures on the walls / Whispering in the halls . . . clean clothes . . . little red shoes' – catching them on the fly as tokens of the many impressions that the receptive consciousness of the speaker / writer is open to. Song after song confronts the world in this way: as a result when reading through the songs we can't help but notice the many things that are recorded: cigarettes, fishing rods, radios, train tracks, shoes, combs, coats, accordions to list just a few of the inanimate kind, a list that can be doubled and redoubled if we move into the natural, the animate, and the human world. As against this impulse there is the contrary one which seeks to bring everything into something like harmony, to abstract from the welter of sense impressions some overarching vision in which a song can be about all things simultaneously. These impulses can be seen as centrifugal and centripetal, forces pulling in opposite directions, and taking our lead from this we can see how Morrison's body of work is marked by a number of similarly oppositional forces. There are the songs that forbid looking back, and the songs steeped in memory; there are the songs that assert the need to dwell in the particular moment and the songs that search for the transcendent; the songs of joy in this world and the songs warning against the material world (including those in which the music business is excoriated). Again this list of oppositions could be continued to encompass the whole body of work. The obvious immediate response to this point is to quote from Walt Whitman (named in 'Rave On, John Donne Part II'): 'Do I contradict myself? / Very well then I contradict myself, / (I am large, I contain multitudes.)' That would certainly be one way of thinking about Morrison's songs as a body of work, but to leave it there would also be a disservice to that work by implying that there is an irresolution at the heart of it. It is better then to consider these various oppositions as foundational contradictions in line with (to take another of Morrison's references) William Blake's 'Without Contraries is no progression.' From very early on the situation of lovers in Morrison's songs echoes this sense of opposition: 'And there go you and I / Between the earth and sky' ('My Lonely Sad Eyes'). In doing so it also slides between sacred and secular forms of love. Of course, in saying this we are pointing not just to Blake (and a number of other writers besides Blake) but also to the traditions of soul, blues and gospel music in which this elision of the sacred and profane is central.

Which brings us to the question of where Van Morrison stands in relation to tradition and how that relates to his undoubted originality. In 'Goldfish Bowl' he refers to 'Jazz, Blues & Funk . . . Folk with a beat / And a little bit of Soul' which is a good starting point (though by no means the destination) for thinking about his relationship to tradition. We tend to see the artist, at least since the period of the Romantics, as a singular, even solitary, figure, forging ahead with their work while ignoring all others. Equally, at least since Ezra Pound insisted in the early twentieth century that his fellow writers should 'make it new', a premium has been placed on the notion of the original and the modern. Both T. S. Eliot and W. B. Yeats argued against Pound and for tradition – as Yeats put it 'even what I alter must seem traditional ... Ancient salt is best packing.' But both also had some difficulties in defining tradition and how the artist relates to it. Academic writing on this subject has tended to stress what is called the 'anxiety of influence': the idea that any artist, to borrow a phrase from James Joyce, 'frets in the shadow' of his or her predecessors.

Van Morrison can be classified, in the available terms, as a 'solo artist', he is a singer, a songwriter, and a musician, but we know that this classification is only part of the story. Van Morrison is also a bandleader, a frequent collaborator with other singers in his live shows (and on *Duets* he works with sixteen other singers), and a singer and musician who has covered a range of others' songs. That last point is worth dwelling on. Surveying Morrison's recorded work it's hard to overlook his practice of covering of songs by other writers which started with Them and has continued throughout his career. This may seem like a strange point with which to introduce a book of Van Morrison's lyrics, but it offers a way into those lyrics.

Without wishing to turn this introduction into an exercise in allusion spotting (others have done a more comprehensive job than would be possible here) it is worth noting that Morrison's songwriting and his covers of others' work are interdependent. For example, when he covers Sister Rosetta Tharpe's 'How Far from God' on *Roll with the Punches* in 2017 it fits comfortably with the songs that he has written on just this subject. At one level this explains why singers pick songs to cover: the chosen song allows them a variant on a familiar form of expression. But there is something else happening here. What also makes the song familiar within the context of Morrison's work is its repeated phrase 'walk and talk' which appears early in Morrison's writing ('If You and I Could Be As Two', 'Sweet Thing') and the activity, if not the actual words, appear in many other songs ('If I Ever Needed Someone', 'Autumn Song'). It's a common enough phrase and it would be foolish to say that it is an allusion to the Tharpe song, but it fits into a larger pattern. Morrison's own songs are steeped in tropes and themes acquired over a lifetime of listening and performing: in 'Foggy Mountain Top' he notes that he has 'been listening to this music / Ever since the age of three'. It seems to be as natural as breathing for him then to begin a song such as 'Give Me My Rapture' with two lines – 'There are strange things happening every day / I hear music up above my head' – which can be confidently identified as allusions to a Sister Rosetta Tharpe song and to a gospel song made famous by her. Given that this is a spiritual song it is not surprising to find a reference to the idea of the 'dark night of the soul' from St John of the Cross later in the lyric. All of these references might well be considered traditional regardless of their source. By making use of them Morrison is then placing himself within a form of music (and within other forms of writing as well) and might be seen as adapting the tradition to make his own plea for spiritual enlightenment. There is a twist to this, however, in that another version of 'Strange Things Happening', by Etta James, is about an altogether more profane and earthy form of rapture, the very temptation that Morrison's song wishes to resist. 'Give Me My Rapture' then, we could say, is traditional but, more importantly, it is so only because it is part of a tradition that Morrison is creating and mobilising within his work. His songs are then a way of walking and talking with tradition.

This is just one example of how Morrison's songs relate to the several traditions from which they derive. Tharpe is an easier, because more limited, example to deal with than some others; the engagements with William Blake or John Lee Hooker, with W. B. Yeats or Hank Williams are much more expansive. It should go without saying, but it is worth stressing, that these engagements are not all one way. These four names would not fit together in any other context than Morrison's work. Morrison, in other words, is not drawing on some existing tradition; rather he is creating, adding to, and modifying his own tradition as he writes. In contrast to some other ideas of tradition and how artists relate to it, Morrison's engagement is confident and generous; it is hard to think of another writer who is so open to naming and sharing sources, models, inspirations. If the radio brought much of this work to his attention, then it's as if his songs have now become an equivalent to the radio from which others can learn. There is little sense here of any anxiety or fretfulness. Instead, there is a joyous cataloguing of predecessors who are celebrated and honoured, treated with generosity and given their due by someone who stands confidently in line with them as an equal, someone who has created his own tradition by creating his own body of work. Steeped though they are in traditions, we never have any doubt that we are hearing a Van Morrison song. Where else would you find William Wordsworth, Lawrence Ferlinghetti and Jon Hendricks being brought together in a way that makes sense. Van Morrison's songs are then a conversation both with himself and with this ever-developing tradition. When he rhymes 'crossroads' with 'arcadian groves'? in 'Pagan Heart' he brings both Robert Johnson and W. B. Yeats into the conversation, and we are reminded that although they are near contemporaries there is nowhere else but in Morrison's work that such a connection would be made. We can therefore look to his work not just for what it does in its own right but also for how it can reshape our sense of cultural connections.

Paradoxically it is this kind of engagement with the tradition that he has created that is one of the most original aspects of Van Morrison's writing. Without him this tradition would not exist. When you get to the final words of this book ('The Prophet Speaks') what you are reading is another part of Van Morrison's life-long conversation with the tradition that he has shaped, not just for himself but for us as well: 'Come closer now / I'll tell you with a whisper'.

Eamonn Hughes
September 2019

If You and I Could Be As Two

It was on a Sunday and the autumn leaves were on the
    ground
Kicked my heart when I saw you standing there in your dress
    of blue
The storm was over, my ship sailed through
What is this feeling, what can I do?

If you and I could be relieved to walk and talk
And be deceived I'd give my all and all
And more I would do
If darling only you and I could be as two

If we could dream and by our dreams
Sew this wicked world up at the seams
I'd give my life, and more I would do
If darling only you and I could be as two

Baby do you remember
All the good times we had together
Walkin' through the park
Baby then, then we could sing
Give you all my money
Everything in the world that I have
You told me that don't mean a thing

If still in darkness
We could run together there
In that morning sun
I'd give my all, my love and everything to you
If darling only you and I could be as two
Could be as two

Could be as two
Could be as two

Bad or Good

Everybody's got some soul
I don't care if they're young or old
Gotta hold on, when all is gone
Make out like it's fine

While we say yeah (bad or good)
Oh Yeah (bad or good)
Yeah, yeah, yeah, yeah, yeah, yeah (bad or good)
Gotta let it happen (bad or good)
Everybody (bad or good)
Sometime, oh yeah

Don't even have to say one word
It ain't nothin that we've seen or heard
Get out, get out, jump back child
Make like you know what it's all about

And we say yeah (bad or good)
Oh Yeah (bad or good)
Oh baby (bad or good)
Gotta let it happen (bad or good)
Everybody (bad or good)
Sometime, some sweet time

If there's something, baby, you want me to do
Come on over here and I'll see about you
Yeah I'll make it, shake it all about
Jump back child

Just say yeah (bad or good)
Oh Yeah (bad or good)

Oh Yeah (bad or good)
Gotta let it happen (bad or good)
Everybody (bad or good)
Sometime, sometime, oh yeah

Could You Would You

Could you, would you, hold me in your arms
Show me all your charms or make me sad or make me blue
Could you love me, like I love you, like I love you?

Could you, would you, squeeze and hold me tight
Love me all through the night, never ever let me go
Could you love me, like I love you so, like I love you so?

Every time I see you walkin' down my avenue
I say hi hi hi hi hi, are you alright?
You say how do you do
Just like you always do
But if I had you in my arms tonight

Could you, would you, hold me oh so near
While I whisper in your ear
The sweet words, you long to hear
Could you love me, like I love you, like I love you?

Could you, would you, hold me oh so near
While I whisper in your ear
The sweet words, you long to hear
Could you love me, like I love you, like I love you,
Just like I love you?

Friday's Child

From the North to the South
You walked all the way
You know you left your home
Left your home for good to stay

While you built all
All your castles in the sun
And I watched you knock 'em down
Knock 'em down, each and every one

Oh, Friday's child, you can't stop now, no
Oh, Friday's child, you can't stop now

And I watched you before you came too old
And I told you, a long time before
You ever came to be told
You got somethin' that they all wanna know
You gotta hold on and never, never let go

Oh, Friday's child, you can't stop now, no, no
Oh, Friday's child, you cannot stop now
You can't stop

There you go,
There you go with rainbows hangin' round your feet
And you're makin' out
You're makin' out with everyone that you meet
You're even having a ball and staying out late
And watched the sun come up round Notting Hill Gate

Oh, Friday's child, you can't stop now, no, no

Oh, Friday's child, you cannot stop, you're driving
No, no, no, no, no, no, no, no, no, no
You cannot stop now,
It's too much
You can't stop
You can't stop
You can't stop

One Two Brown Eyes

Went out last night walkin'
I heard someone talkin'
You'd better stop stayin' out late at night
Straighten up and fight
Right you better stop tellin' those lies
Gonna cut you down to my size
You got one, you got two brown eyes
Hypnotize, hypnotize, hypnotize
Yeah, Yeah, oh
Oh, oh, oh, oh,
Oh, oh, oh, oh

You got such pretty good looks
You don't really find in good books
You'd better stop staying out late at night
Or straighten up and fight, right
I gonna cut you down to my size
You got one, two brown eyes
Hypnotize
Oh what eyes
Hypnotize
Yeah, yeah, oh
Oh, oh, oh, oh,
Oh, oh, oh, oh

You Just Can't Win

One more coffee, one more cigarette
One more morning trying to forget
If I had a chance to join your dance
I wouldn't like to bet your game is something

Yet it's a shame
Ain't natural for you
Baby it's a sin
You know you just can't win
When you are in

You used to ride on buses
Take a tube to Camden Town
Now you go by aeroplane
Don't let nothing bring you down

Yet it's a shame
Ain't natural for you
Baby it's a sin
You know you just can't win
When you are in

Now the road is dark and lonely
But you got to bear the load
You're up in Park Lane now
I'm somewhere round the Tottenham Court Road

Yet it's a shame
Ain't natural for you
Baby it's a sin
You know you just can't win

When you are in

No, you just can't win
No, you just can't win
When you are in

The Smile You Smile

The smile you smile is you
And I see through your laughing eyes
The smile you smile is you
And I see through your laughing eyes, oh baby
And in the whirlpool of them
I can be in paradise

And I'd go roamin' in the gloamin'
Ever and a day with you,
I'd go roamin' in the gloamin'
Ever and a day with you
And sit between the stars and say
That that's my point of view

I-I-I-I-I love you
I-I-I-I-I love you

And talk to trees and sunshine
Feel your lips against my lip
And talk to trees and sunshine
Feel your lips against my lip
And smell your sweet perfume
And even touch your fingertips

I-I-I-I-I love you
I-I-I-I-I love you
I-I-I-I-I love you

Astral Weeks

If I ventured in the slipstream
Between the viaducts of your dreams
Where immobile steel rims crack
And the ditch in the back roads stop

Could you find me
Would you kiss my eyes
And lay me down in the silence easy
To be born again, to be born again?

Far from the side of the ocean
If I put the wheels in motion
And I stand with my arms behind me
And I pushed another door

Could you find me
Would you kiss my eyes
Lay me down in the silence easy
To be born again, to be born again?

There you go standing with the look of Avarice
Talking to Huddie Ledbetter
Showing pictures on the walls
Whispering in the halls
And pointing a finger at me

There you go, there you go
Standing in the sun darling
With your arms behind you
And your eyes before

There you go
Taking care of your boy
Seeing that he's got clean clothes
Putting on his little red shoes
Seeing that he's got clean clothes
Putting on his little red shoes
Pointing a finger at me

And here I am
Standing in your sad arrest
Trying to do my very best
Looking straight at you
And coming through, darling

If I ventured in the slipstream
Between the viaducts of your dreams
Where immobile steel rims crack
And the ditch in the back roads stop

Could you find me
Would you kiss my eyes
And lay me down in the silence easy
To be born again, to be born again?

To be born again, to be born again

In another world, darling
In another world
In another time
Got a home on high

Ain't nothing but a stranger in this world
I'm nothing but a stranger in this world
I got a home on high
In another land so far away, so far away

Way up in the heaven
Way up in the heaven
Way up in the heaven
Way up in the heaven

In another time
In another place
In another time
In another place
Way up in the heaven
In another time
In another place
In another time
In another place
And another face

Sweet Thing

And I shall stroll the merry way and jump the hedges first
And I will drink clear clean water for to quench my thirst
And I shall watch the ferry boats and they'll get high
On a blue ocean against tomorrow's sky

And I will never grow so old again
And I will walk and talk in gardens all wet with rain
Oh, oh, oh sweet thing
Sweet thing, sweet thing
Oh, my, my, my sweet thing

I shall drive my chariot down your streets and cry
'Well it's me and I'm dynamite and I don't know why'
And you shall take me strongly in your arms again
And I wonder if I might remember that I ever felt the pain

We shall walk and talk in gardens all misty wet
All misty wet with rain down on
And I will never, never, never grow so old again
Oh, oh sweet thing
Oh, oh, oh you sweet thing
Sweet thing
My, my, my,

And I will raise my hands up into the nighttime sky
And count the stars that's shining in your eye
And just to dig it all not to wonder that's just right
And I'll be satisfied not to read in between the lines

And I will walk and talk in gardens all wet with rain
And I will never ever, ever, ever grow so old again

Oh, oh sweet thing
Oh, oh, oh, sugar baby
Oh, oh, sweet thing
Sugar baby
Sugar baby
Sugar baby
What a champagne eye
And your sweet light smile

And It Stoned Me

Half a mile from the county fair
And the rain came pourin' down
Me and Billy standin' there
With a silver half a crown
Hands are full of fishin' rod
And the tackle on our backs
We just stood there gettin' wet
With our backs against the fence

Oh, the water
Oh, the water
Oh, the water
Hope it don't rain all day

And it stoned me to my soul
Stoned me just like Jelly Roll
And it stoned me
And it stoned me to my soul
Stoned me just like goin' home
And it stoned me

And the rain let up and the sun came up
And we were getting' dry
Almost let a pick-up truck nearly pass us by
So we jumped right in and the driver grinned
And he dropped us up the road
And we looked at the swim and we jumped right in
Not to mention fishing poles

Oh, the water
Oh, the water

Oh, the water
Let it run all over me

And it stoned me to my soul
Stoned me just like Jelly Roll
And it stoned me
And it stoned me to my soul
Stoned me just like goin' home
And it stoned me

On the way back home we sang a song
But our throats were getting dry
Then we saw the man from across the road
With the sunshine in his eye
Well he lived all alone in his own little home
With a great big gallon jar
There were bottles too, one for me and you
And he said, 'Hey, there you are.'

Oh, the water
Oh, the water
Oh, the water
Get it myself from the mountain stream

And it stoned me to my soul
Stoned me just like Jelly Roll
And it stoned me
And it stoned me to my soul
Stoned me just like goin' home
And it stoned me
And it stoned me to my soul
Stoned me just like Jelly Roll
And it stoned me
And it stoned me to my soul
Stoned me just like goin' home
And it stoned me

Crazy Love

I can hear her heart beat from a thousand miles
And the heavens open every time she smiles
And when I come to her that's where I belong
Yet I'm running to her like a river song

She give me love, love, love, love, crazy love
She give me love, love, love, love, crazy love

She got a fine sense of humour when I'm feeling low down
And when I come to her when the sun goes down
Take away my trouble, take away my grief
Take away my heartache, in the night like a thief

She give me love, love, love, love, crazy love
She give me love, love, love, love, crazy love

Yeah I need her in the daytime
Yeah I need her in the night
Yeah I want to throw my arms around her
And kiss her hug her kiss and hug her tight

And when I'm returning from so far away
She give me some sweet lovin' brighten up my day
And it make me righteous, and it make me whole
And it make me mellow down to my soul

She give me love, love, love, love, crazy love
She give me love, love, love, love, crazy love
She give me love, love, love, love, crazy love
She give me love, love, love, love, crazy love

Caravan

And the caravan is on its way
I can hear the merry gypsy play
Mama, mama look at Ammaro
She's a-playing with the radio
La, la, la, la, la, la, la
La, la, la, la, la, la, la

And the caravan has all my friends
It will stay with me until the end
Gypsy Robin, Sweet Ammaro
Tell me everything I need to know
La, la, la, la, la, la, la
La, la, la, la, la, la, la

Turn up your radio and let me hear the song
Switch on your electric light
Then we can get down to what is really wrong
I long to hold you tight so I can feel you
Sweet lady of the night I shall reveal you

If you will
Turn it up, turn it up, little bit higher, radio
Turn it up, burn it up, so you know, radio
La, la, la, la, la, la, la
La, la, la, la, la, la, la

And the caravan is painted red and white
That means everybody's staying overnight
And the barefoot gypsy boy round the campfire sing and play
And a woman tells us of her way

La, la, la, la, la, la, la
La, la, la, la, la, la, la

Turn up the radio and let me hear the song
Switch on your electric light
Then we can get down to what is really wrong
I long just to hold you tight so baby I can feel you
Sweet lady of the night I shall reveal you

If you will
Turn it up, turn it up, little bit higher, radio
Turn it up, that's enough, so you know it's got soul
Radio, radio, turn it up,
La, la, la, la, la, la, la, la, la, la, la, la, la, la

Come Running

By the side of the tracks where the train goes by
The wind and the rain will catch you, you will sigh
Deep in your heart
Then you'll come running to me
You'll come running to me

Well you watch the train go round the bend
Play in dust and dream that it will never end
Deep in your heart
You'll come running to me
You'll come running to me

Said, hey, come running to me
Oh, come running to me
Hey, yeah, come running to me
Said, hey, come running to me
Oh, come running to me
Hey, yeah, come running to me

With your hound dog by your side
And your arms stretched out open wide
I wanna keep you satisfied in the morning sun
By my side, come on, come on run

Well alright hey, in the country
Kick the sand up with your heels
You think to yourself how good it feels
Put away all your walking shoes
Then you come running to me
Hey, yeah, now you come running to me

I said, hey, come running to me
Oh, come running to me
Hey, yeah, come running to me
Hey, come running to me
Oh, come running to me
Hey, yeah, come running to me
Come on, come on, run
Come on run
Come on run
Come on run
Come running
Come on
Run to me

You gotta rainbow if you run to me

These Dreams of You

I dreamed you paid your dues in Canada
And left me to come through
I headed for there right way
I knew exactly just what to do
I dreamed we played cards in the dark
And you lost and you lied
Wasn't very hard to do
But hurt me deep down inside

These dreams of you
So real and so true
These dreams of you
So real and so true

My back was up against the wall
And you slowly just walked away
You never really heard my call
When I cried out that way
With my face against the sun
You pointed out for me to go
Then you said I was the one
Had to reap what you did sow

These dreams of you
So real and so true
These dreams of you
So real and so true

And hush-a-bye, don't ever think about it
Go to sleep and don't ever say one word
Close your eyes, you are an angel sent here from above

And Ray Charles was shot down
But he got up to do his best
A crowd of people gathered round
To the question answered, 'yes'
And you slapped me on the face
I turned around the other cheek
You couldn't really stand the pace
And I would never be so meek

These dreams of you
So real and so true
These dreams of you
So real and so true

And hush-a-bye, hush-a-bye don't ever think about it
Go to sleep, don't ever say one word
Close your eyes, you are an angel sent here from above
And hush-a-bye, hush-a-bye don't ever think about it
Go to sleep, don't ever say one word
Close your eyes

Everyone

We shall walk again, all along the lane
Down the avenue just like we used to
With our heads held high smile at passers by
Then we'll softly sigh ay, yi, yi, yi, yi, yi

Everyone, everyone, everyone, everyone
Everyone, everyone, everyone, everyone

By the winding stream we shall lay and dream
And make dreams come true if we want them to
And so overcome play the pipes and drum
Sing a happy song and we'll sing along

Everyone, everyone, everyone, everyone
Everyone, everyone, everyone, everyone

We shall walk again all along down the lane
Down the avenue just like we used to
With our heads held high smile at passers by
Then we'll softly sigh ay, yi, yi, yi, yi, yi

Everyone, everyone, everyone, everyone
Everyone, everyone, everyone, everyone

Domino

Don't want to discuss it
I think it's time for a change
You may get disgusted
Start thinking that I'm strange
In that case I'll go underground
Get some heavy rest
Never have to worry
About what is worst and what is best

I said, Oh, Oh Domino
Roll me over, Romeo
Lord have mercy, I said
Oh, Oh Domino
Roll me over, Romeo, there you go
Say it again, I said
Oh, Oh Domino
I said Oh, Oh Domino

There's no need for argument
There's no argument at all
And if you never hear from him
That just means he didn't call
Or vice versa
That depends on wherever you're at
And if you never hear from me
That just means I would rather not

Oh, Oh Domino
Roll me over, Romeo
There you go
Lord have mercy, I said

Oh, Oh Domino
Roll me over Romeo
There you go
Say it again
Oh, Oh Domino
I said Oh, Oh Domino

Hey Mr DJ
I just want to hear some rhythm and blues music
On the radio
On the radio
On the radio

Virgo Clowns

Let us free you from the pain
Let us see you smile again
Let us unlock all the chains
You're broken hearted

Let us help you to forget
Let us help you unlock it
It's not nearly time to quit
You've only started

You gotta
Sit down funny face
Let your laughter fill the room
Light up your golden smile
Take away all your misery and gloom
Let your laughter fill the room
Let your laughter fill the room

Let us shake you by the hand
Let us help you understand
Take your head out of the sand
And shake it free now

Let us help you to go on
We are here to lean upon
Now you know exactly just who
You want to be now

Sit down funny face
Let your laughter, let your laughter fill the room
Light up your golden smile

Take away all your misery and gloom
Let your laughter fill the room
Let your laughter fill the room

Let us lift you up on high
See the twinkle in your eye
Raise you up into the sky
And say it's easy

Hey let the trumpets ring it
Let the angels sing it
Let your pretty feet go dancing
Let your worn out mind go prancing
Sit down funny face
Let your laughter fill the room
Light up your golden smile
Take away all your misery and gloom
Let your laughter fill the room
Let your laughter fill the room
Let your laughter fill the room
Let your laughter fill the room
Let it fill the room
Let it fill the room
Let your laughter fill the room

If I Ever Needed Someone

Lord if I ever needed someone I need you
Lord if I ever needed someone I need you

To see me through the daytime
And through the long lonely night
To lead me through the darkness
And on into the light
To stand with me when I'm troubled
And help me through my strife
When times get so uncertain to turn to you
Turn to you in my young life

Lord if I ever needed someone I need you
Lord if I ever needed someone I need you

Someone to hold on to
And keep me from all fear
Someone to be my guiding light
And keep me ever dear
To keep me from my selfishness
To keep me from my sorrow
To lead me on to givingness
So I can see a new tomorrow

Lord if I ever needed someone I need you
Lord if I ever needed someone I need you

Someone to walk with
Someone to hold by the hand
Someone to talk with
Someone to understand

To call on when I need you
And I need you very much
To open up my arms to you
And feel your tender touch
To feel it and to keep it
Just right here in my soul
And care for it and keep it with me
Never to grow old

Lord if I ever needed someone I need you
Lord if I ever needed someone I need you
Lord if I ever needed someone I need you
Lord if I ever needed someone I need you

Wild Night

As you brush your shoes
And stand before the mirror
And you comb your hair
Grab your coat and hat
And you walk wet streets
Tryin' to remember
All the wild night breezes
In your memory ever.

And everything looks so complete
When you're walkin' out on the street
And the wind catches your feet
And sends you flyin', cryin'
Oooh-wee
The wild night is calling
Oooh-wee
The wild night is calling

And all the girls walk by
Dressed up for each other
And the boys do the boogie-woogie
On the corner of the street
And the people passin' by
Just stare in wild wonder
And the inside juke-box
Roars out just like thunder.

And everything looks so complete
When you walk out on the street
And the wind catches your feet
And sends you flyin', cryin'

Oooh-wee
The wild night is calling
Oooh-wee
The wild night is calling

The wild night is calling
The wild night is calling
Come on out and dance
Come on out and make romance
Come on out and dance
Come on out and make romance

The wild night is calling
The wild night is calling
Come on out and dance
Come on out and make romance
Come on out and dance
Come on out and make romance

I Wanna Roo You (Scottish Derivative)

Twenty third of December, covered in snow
You in the kitchen with the lights way down low
I'm in the parlour playing my old guitar
Speaking to you, darling, find out how you are
I wanna roo you, wanna get through to you
I wanna woo you, woo you tonight
I wanna roo you, wanna get through to you
I wanna woo you, woo you tonight

Come to me softly, come to me quiet
Know what I'm after and I'm gonna try it
Snowstorm's on the way and we'll be stranded for a week
Come over to the window, look outside take a peek
I wanna roo you, wanna get through to you
I wanna woo you, woo you tonight
I wanna roo you, wanna get through to you
I wanna woo you, woo you tonight

You know I am lonely and in need of your company
Oh, let your love light shine on down on me

And we can just sit here, look at the fire
Watch the flames leaping higher and higher
Tea on the stove, food in the pan
Ain't going nowhere and we don't have many plans
I wanna roo you, wanna get through to you
I wanna woo you, woo you tonight
I wanna roo you, wanna get through to you
I wanna woo you, woo you tonight

And you know I am lonely

I been in need of your company
Let your love, let your love this morning
Shine on down on me
I wanna roo you, wanna get through to you
I wanna woo you, woo you tonight
I wanna roo you, wanna get through to you
I wanna woo you, woo you tonight
Woo you tonight, pretty baby
Woo you tonight, little darling
Woo you tonight, it's alright
Woo you tonight

I Will Be There

Whenever the sunshine comes through
Whenever my thoughts turn to you
Whatever you want me to do
I will be there

Whether I crawled up the hill
Child you know I've been through the mill
Just as long as I fit the bill
I will be there

If it's on a lazy afternoon in summertime
And you're drinkin' champagne and wine
Any time I don't mind
And even if I've got the blues
After I've paid all my dues
And you decide to go for a cruise
I will be there

And If it's on a lazy afternoon in summertime
And you're drinkin' champagne and wine
Any time I don't mind
And even if I've got the blues
On account of paying oh so many dues
And you decide to go for a cruise

Gonna grab my razor and my suitcase
And my toothbrush, and my overcoat
And my underwear
I will be there

Redwood Tree

Boy and his dog
Went out looking for the rainbow
And oh, what did they learn
Since that very day

Walking by the river
And running like a blue streak
Through the fields and streams and meadows
Laughing all the way

Oh Redwood Tree
Please let us under
When we were young we used to go
Under the Redwood Tree

And it smells like rain
Maybe even thunder
Won't you keep us from all harm
Wonderful Redwood Tree

And a boy and his father
Went out, went out looking for the lost dog
And oh what, oh what have they learned
Since they did that together

They did not bring him back
He already had departed
But look at everything they have learned
Since that, since that very day

Oh Redwood Tree

Please let us under
When we were young we used to go
Under the Redwood Tree

And it smells like rain
Maybe even thunder
Won't you keep us from all harm
Wonderful Redwood Tree

Autumn Song

Leaves of brown they fall to the ground
And it's here, over there leaves abound
Shut the door dim the lights and relax
What is more, your desire, or the facts

Pitter patter the rain falling down
Little glimmer sun coming round
Take a walk when autumn comes to town

Little stroll past the house on the hill
Some more coal on the fire if you will
And in a week or two it'll be Halloween
Set the page and the stage for the scene

Little game the children will play
And as we watch them while time away
Look at me and take my breath away

You'll be smiling eyes beguiling
And the song on the breeze
Will call my name out
In your dreams

Chestnuts roasting outside as you walk
With your love by your side
The old accordion man plays mellow
and bright
And you go home in the crispness of
the night

Little later friends will be along

And if you feel like joining the throng
Just might feel like singing autumn song
Just may feel like

You'll be smiling
Eyes beguiling
And the song on the breeze
Calls my name out in your dreams

Chestnuts roasting outside
As you walk with your love by your side
And the old accordion man plays mellow, mellow and bright
And you go home in the crispness of the night

Little later friends will be along
And if you feel like joining the throng
Just might feel like singing autumn song
Just may feel like singing autumn song

You just may break out
You just may break out
You just may
You just may have to break out
You just may
You just may have to lose control
You just may have to lose control
'Cause you got it in your soul
You just may
Just may have to break out
You just may
You just may have to break out

Break out
Hear what I'm singing
Way out in the distance

Way out in the distance
Way over in the corner
Way out in the distance
Cable car
And I hear the church bells chime
And I hear the church bells chime
Way out in the distance
Way out in the distance
Infinitesimal
Beauty of your eyes
Catches me in my starlight
Gazing, gazing
And I'm embracing something
Turn around
Hand on my shoulder
Saying
It's so peaceful
It's so peaceful
Inside
Inside
Inside
I believe I've
I believe I've
Transcended myself child
Transcended myself child
Transcended myself child

Mechanical Bliss

Mechanical bliss is striking me for what I believe in
The ribbon on the line, and getting in and getting out
Was not like this

No, mechanical bliss was not like this at all

The ribbon on the line, and getting in and getting out
Was not like this, was not like this, was not like this

Caruthers and Smith said that they couldn't come at all

They said that their backs were up against the wall

And getting in and getting out
Was not like this, was not like this, was not like this

But a flash of the list, the flick of a switch

A flick of a switch, you gave me a kiss, I couldn't resist
No, mechanical bliss

Now Ponsonby-Smith said he really didn't care

About Neville and Chippy who really wasn't there

And getting in and getting out
Was not like this, was not like this

He's out in the sun, he's sucking his thumb

He's talking to Hun

Oh, mechanical bliss

Mechanical bliss was not like this
Mechanical bliss was not like this at all

The ribbon on the line and getting in and getting out
Was not like this, was never, never like this

I couldn't resist the flash of the list, a flick of the switch
The lisp, you talked in a lisp, you gave me a kiss

You talked in a lisp, you talked in a lisp
Mechanical bliss

O.K. Chaps, stiff upper lip!

Fair Play

Fair play to you
Killarney's lakes are so blue
And the architecture I'm taking in with my mind
Is so fine

Tell me of Poe
Oscar Wilde and Thoreau
Let your midnight and your daytime
Turn into love of life

It's a very fine line
But you've got the mind child
To carry it on when it's just about to be carried on

And there's only one meadows way to go
And you say Geronimo
And there's only one meadows way to go
And you say Geronimo

A paperback book as we walk down the street
Fill my mind with tales of mystery, mystery
And imagination
Forever fair
And I'm touching your hair
I wish we would be dreamers in this dream
Oh, oh let it be

And there's only one meadows way to go
And you say Geronimo
And there's only one meadows way to go
And you say Geronimo

Fair play to you
Killarney's lakes are so blue
Hi ho silver tit for tat
And I love you for that

Hi ho silver tit for tat
And I love you for that
Love you for that
Love you for that
Hi ho silver tit for tat
Tit for tat
And I love you for that
Hi ho silver tit for tat
And I love you for that

And there's only one meadows way to go
And I say Geronimo
And there's only one meadows way to go
And we say Geronimo, Geronimo

And there's only one meadows way to go
And we say Geronimo
And there's only one meadows way to go
And we say Geronimo

Fair play to you

Linden Arden Stole the Highlights

Linden Arden stole the highlights
With one hand tied behind his back
Loved the moon and sun and whiskey
Ran like water in his veins

Loved to go to church on Sunday
Even though he was a drinkin' man
When the boys came to San Francisco
They were lookin' for his life

But he found out where they were drinkin'
Met them face to face outside
Cleaved their heads off with a hatchet
Lord he was a drinkin' man

And when somebody tried to get above him
He just took the law into his own hands
Linden Arden stole the highlights
And he put his fingers through the glass

He had heard all the stories many, many times before
And he did not care no more to ask
And he loved the little children
Like they were his very own

He said say some day it may get lonely
Now he's living, living with a gun

Who Was That Masked Man?

Oh ain't it lonely when you're living with a gun
Well you can't slow down and you can't turn around
And you can't trust anyone

You just sit there like a butterfly
And you're all encased in glass
You're so fragile you just may break
And ya don't know who to ask

Oh ain't it lonely when you're living with a gun
Well you can't slow down and you can't turn around
And you can't trust anyone

You just sit there like a butterfly
You're well protected by the glass
You're such a rare collector's item
When they throw away what's trash

You can hang suspended from a star
Wish on a toilet roll
You can just soak up the atmosphere
Like a fish inside a bowl

When the ghost comes round at midnight
Well you both can have some fun
He can drive you mad, he can make you sad
He can keep you from the sun

When they take him down he'll both be safe and sound
And the hand does fit the glove
And no matter what they tell you
There's good and evil in everyone

Streets of Arklow

And as we walked
Through the streets of Arklow
Oh the colour
Of the day wore on
And our heads
Were filled with poetry
In the morning
A-comin' on to dawn

And as we walked
Through the streets of Arklow
In gay profusion
In God's green land
And the gypsies rode
With their hearts on fire
They say 'We love to wander,
Lord we love,
Lord we love to roam.'

And as we walked
Through the streets of Arklow
In all its raging beauty
Rolling back to the day
And I saw your eyes
They was shining, sparkling crystal clear
And our souls were clean
As the grass did grow
And our souls were clean
As the grass did grow
And our souls were clean
As the grass did grow

And as we walked
Through the streets of Arklow

You Don't Pull No Punches but You Don't Push the River

When you were a child, you were a tomboy
Gimme soul satisfaction
Way back in shady lane
Do you remember darlin'

And it's the woman in you, and it's the woman in you
Gimme soul satisfaction
And it takes the child in you to know
The woman an' you are one

We're goin' out in the country to get down to the real soul,
I mean the real soul, people,
We're talkin about real soul people
We're goin' out in the country, get down to the real soul
We're gettin' in to the west coast
Shining our light into the days of bloomin' wonder
Goin' as much with the river as not, as not,
An' I'm goin' as much with the river as not

Blake and the Eternals, standin' with the Sisters of Mercy
Looking for the Veedon Fleece,
William Blake and the Eternals, standin' with the Sisters of
    Mercy
Looking for the Veedon Fleece.

You don't pull no punches, but you don't push the river
You don't pull no punches, and you don't push the river
You don't pull no punches, and you don't push the river, no,
    no
Goin' as much with the river as not

We're goin' out in the West, down to the cathedrals
We're goin' out in the West, down to the beaches
And the Sisters of Mercy, behind the sun
Oh behind the sun

And William Blake and the Sisters of Mercy looking for the
    Veedon Fleece,
You don't pull no punches, goin' West, goin' as much with
    the river as not
With the river as not, with the river as not, goin' as much,
Goin' as much with the river as not, no,
You don't pull no punches, and you don't push the river, no
You don't pull no punches, but you don't push the river, no
You don't pull no punches, but you don't push the river, no
You don't pull no punches, but you don't push the river

And we was contemplating Baba, William Blake and the
    Eternals
Goin' down to the Sisters of Mercy
Looking for the Veedon Fleece
Looking for the Veedon Fleece
Looking for the Veedon Fleece

You don't pull no punches, but ya, you don't push the river
You don't pull no punches, but ya, you don't push the river,
    no
You don't pull no punches, but ya, you don't push the river
You don't push the river, you don't push the river

You Gotta Make It through the World

Well let them take you for a clown
And they're bound to bring you down
You got to make it through the world if you can
Think they're doing you wrong
But you got here on your own
You got to make it through the world if you can
I said if you can, if you can
You got to make it through the world if you can
I said if you can, if you can
You got to make it through the world if you can

Well you know without a doubt
Nobody know you when you're down and out
You got to make it through the world if you can
Well talk about wrong and right
You've got to make up your own mind
You got to make it through the world if you can

I said if you can, if you can
You got to make it through the world if you can
I said if you can, well if you can
You got to make it through the world if you can

Yeah, let them take you for a clown
They will surely put you down
You got to make it through the world if you can
Everybody talk about wrong and right
You got to make up your own mind about it
You got to make it through the world if you can

Oh, if you can, if you can
You got to make it through the world if you can

Yeah, if you can, if you can
You got to make it through the world if you can
Yeah I said if you can, Lord, if you can
You got to make it through the world if you can

I said you got to make through the world if you can
I said you got to make through the world if you can
I said you got to make through the world if you can
You got to make it through the world if you can

Make it through the world
Make it through the world
Make it through the world
Make it through the world
Make it through the world
Got to make it through the world

The Eternal Kansas City

Excuse me do you know the way to Kansas City?
Excuse me do you know the way to Kansas City?
Excuse me do you know the way to Kansas City?
Excuse me do you know the way to Kansas City?

Train down to St Louis in Missouri
Over to the city there, you know that one
Where the farmer's daughter digs the farmer's son
Dig your Charlie Parker
Basie and Young
Witherspoon and Jay McShann
It will come

Excuse me do you know the way to Kansas City?
Excuse me do you know the way to Kansas City?
Excuse me do you know the way to Kansas City?
Excuse me do you know the way to Kansas City?

Lady Liberty is waiting
You know she lights the way
Her name is Billie, she's a Holiday
And the city is eternal, can't you see?
It's inside of you and it's inside of me

You know, you know the way to Kansas City
You know, you know the way to Kansas City
You know, you know the way to Kansas City
You know, you know the way to Kansas City
You know, the way to Kansas City
You know, the way to Kansas City
Wham-Bam

(You know the way to Kansas City)
Thank you Ma'am
(You know the way to Kansas City)
Sing it
You know the way to Kansas City
Hey
You know the way to Kansas City
You know the way to Kansas City
You know the way to Kansas City
You know the way to Kansas City
You know
The way to Kansas City one time

(You know the way to Kansas City)
(You know the way to Kansas City)
(You know the way to Kansas City)
(You know the way to Kansas City)
(You know the way to Kansas City)

Joyous Sound

How sweet that joyous sound
Whenever we meet, whenever we meet
How sweet that joyous sound
Whenever we meet again

I think you'll know it well
Whenever we meet, whenever we meet
I think you'll know it well
Whenever we meet again

Just let it in and let it out
And you will begin to know without a doubt

That grace will follow us
Wherever we go, wherever we go
That grace will follow us
Until we meet again

Just let it in and let it out
And you will begin to know without a doubt

That grace will follow us
Wherever we go, wherever we go
That grace will follow us
Until we meet again

How sweet that joyous sound
Whenever we meet, whenever we meet
How sweet that joyous sound
Whenever we meet again
Whenever we meet

Whenever we meet
Whenever we meet again
Whenever we meet
Whenever we meet
Whenever we meet again
Whenever we meet
Whenever we meet
Whenever we meet again

Flamingos Fly

Go for a ride
In the still of the night
And morning brings forth
All its wonderful delight
Couldn't have made it more plain
When I heard that soft refrain
And I heard you gently sigh

Wanna take you where flamingos fly, flamingos fly
Way over yonder in the clear blue sky
That's where flamingos fly

Lie in the dark
With the sound of the nightingale
Listen for a lark
I will tell you a tale
Breeze is blowin', blowin' outside
Wanna take that moonlight ride
When I heard you gently sigh

Wanna take you where flamingos fly, flamingos fly
Way over yonder in the clear blue sky
That's where flamingos fly

Well we're here and we're waiting
For that morning light to shine
And I'm looking at you, looking at me, looking right back at
    you
And I'm anticipating signs along the way
Looking at you, looking at me, looking right back at you

I'll follow the road
That will take me, take me right back home
And carry that load
Where the deer and the provincial angels roam
Happiness touches, touches me now
I know where it came from and how
When I heard you gently sigh

Wanna take you where flamingos fly, flamingos fly
Way over yonder in the clear blue sky
That's where flamingos fly, flamingos fly
Way over the rooftops of the houses
I heard it one time, I heard it one time in a lullaby
I heard it one time, I heard it one time in a lullaby
Somewhere, somewhere, somewhere
Way over the rooftops of the houses
Heard it one time in a lullaby
Heard it one time, heard it one time in a lullaby

Checkin' It Out

We've got to put our heads together
I'm sure that we can work it out
I'm weighin' up the situation
And checkin' it out
Takin' it further
Takin' it further
Checkin' it out

This is a workin' situation
I'm tellin' you without a doubt
We've gotta pull it all in tight, baby
Checkin' it out
Takin' it further
Takin' it further
Checkin' it out

And all the obstacles along the way
Sometimes may feel so tremendous
There are guides and spirits all along the way
Who will befriend us

Let's talk it out across the table
Make sure that we leave nothin' out
Get in to it like a meditation
Start checkin' it out
Takin' it further
Takin' it further
Checkin' it out

And all the obstacles along the way
Sometimes may feel so tremendous

There are guides and spirits all along the way
Who will befriend us

Let's talk it out across the table
Make sure that we leave nothin' out
Get in to it like a meditation
Start checkin' it out
Takin' it further
Takin' it further
Checkin' it out

Checkin' it out, now baby
Checkin' it out, checkin' it out
You meditate, you meditate
You meditate
And you come back, you come back
You bring it up now baby
You bring it up now baby
You bring it up
You bring it up now
In your loving cup

Natalia

I'm walkin' down the street
I'm on that midnight beat
I'm on a lonely avenue
Baby, won't you walk with me
Baby, won't you talk with me
Oh, that's all I want you to do, now
Walk with me
Talk to me
Call your name out

Na Na, Na Na, Na Na
Na Na, Na Na, Na Na
Na Na, Na Na, Na Na Natalia

Here on a summer night
I wanna kiss and hold you tight
Just the way we used to do
Walkin' down the same old street
People that we used to meet
Such a long, long time ago, now
Walk with me
Talk to me
And I call out your name

Na Na, Na Na, Na Na
Na Na, Na Na, Na Na
Na Na, Na Na, Na Na Natalia
Na Na, Na Na, Na Na
Na Na, Na Na, Na Na
Na Na, Na Na, Na Na Natalia
On a magic night like this

I hunger for your kiss
On a magic night like this

Na Na, Na Na, Na Na
Na Na, Na Na, Na Na
Na Na, Na Na, Na Na Natalia
Na Na, Na Na, Na Na
Na Na, Na Na, Na Na
Na Na, Na Na, Na Na Natalia

Walk with me
Talk with me
Walk with me
Talk with me
Walk with me
Talk with me
Walk with me
Talk with me
Walk with me baby
Talk with me

Natalia, Natalia, Natalia
Natalia, Natalia, Natalia

Lifetimes

You sit in silence
And the river answers
And I have loved you many, many years
I saw you standing by the wondrous river
And I have come today
To calm your fears

Those lifetimes
So many lifetimes
With you

The boatman singin' far across the water
What is this feelin' in my heart and soul
The nighttime angel spreads her wings
Around me
And I feel the sadness
And the river flows

Those lifetimes
So many lifetimes
With you

Listen to the music inside
That is all that you have to do
Listen to the music inside
Can't you hear what it says to you

And I shall get to know you
In these lifetimes
In awe and wonder
On down through the years

The nighttime angel spreads her wings
Around me
I feel the silence
And my doubts are cleared

Those lifetimes
So many lifetimes
With you

Listen to the music inside
That is all that you have to do now
Listen to the music inside
Can't you hear what it says to you

Listen to the music inside
That is all that you have to do now
Listen to the music inside
Can't you hear what it says to you

Listen to the music inside
Can't you hear
Can't you hear what it says to you
Can't you hear what it says to you now
You gotta sit right down
Sit right down and listen to the music inside
That is all, that is all, that is all, that is all
That you have to do now
Listen, listen, listen
To the music, the music
The music, the music
That is all that you have to do

Hungry for Your Love

I'm hungry for your love
I'm hungry for your love
I'm hungry for your love
But I can wait now

I'm on the telephone
And I am all alone
I'm on the telephone
And we're connected

I got such a lot of love
I wanna give it to you
I got such a lot of love
I wanna give it to you
I got such a lot of love
I wanna give it to you

And though we're far apart
You are here in my heart
And though we're far apart
You're part of me now

And after all the years
And after all the tears
And after all the tears
There's just the truth now

I got such a lot of love
I wanna give it to you
I got such a lot of love
I wanna give it to you

I got such a lot of love
I wanna give it to you

Well, I'm hungry for your love
Hungry for your love
Well, I'm hungry, yeah, well, I'm hungry
For your love now

I love you in buckskin, yeah, yeah
I love you in buckskin, yeah, yeah
I love you, I love you, I love you, I love you
I love you, I love you, I love you, I love you
I love you, I love you, I love you

I'm hungry for your love

Take It Where You Find It

Men saw the stars at the edge of the sea
They thought great thoughts about liberty
Poets wrote down words that did fit
Writers wrote books
Thinkers thought about it

Take it where you find it
Can't leave it alone
You will find a purpose
To carry it on
Mainly when you find it
Your heart will be strong
About it

Many's the road I have walked upon
Many's the hour between dusk and dawn
Many's the time
Many's the mile
I see it all now
Through the eyes of a child

Take it where you find it
Can't leave it alone
You will find a purpose
To carry it on
Mainly when you find it
Your heart will be strong
About it

Lost dreams and found dreams
In America

In America
In America
Lost dreams and found dreams
In America
In America
In America

And close your eyes
Leave it all for a while
Leave the world
And your worries behind
You will build on whatever is real
And wake up each day
To the new waking dream

Take it where you find it
Can't leave it alone
You will find a purpose
To carry it on
Mainly when you find it
Your heart will be strong
About it

Lost dreams and found dreams
In America
In America
In America
Lost dreams and found dreams
In America
In America
In America

Change come over
Talkin' about a change
Change come over

Change come over
Change come over
Change, change, change
Change, change, change
Change, change, change
I'm talkin' about a
Change, change, change
Change, change, change
Change come over
Sing it to me now

I'm gonna walk down the street
Until I see
My shining light
I'm gonna walk down the street
Until I see
My shining light
I'm gonna walk down the street
Until I see
My shining light
I'm gonna walk down the street
Until I see
My shining light
Here it comes
I see my light
See my light
See my shining light
I see my light
See my light
I see my shining light
I see my light
See my light
See my shining light
I see my light
See my light

See my shining light

Lost dreams and found dreams
In America
In America
In America
Lost dreams and found dreams
In America
In America
In America
Lost dreams and found dreams
In America
In America
In America
Lost dreams and found dreams
In America
In America
In America

Full Force Gale

Like a full force gale
I was lifted up again
I was lifted up again by the Lord

No matter where I roam
I will find my way back home
I will always return to the Lord

In the gentle evening breeze
By the whispering shady trees
I will find my sanctuary in the Lord

I was heading for a fall
And I saw the writing on the wall

Like a full force gale
I was lifted up again
I was lifted up again by the Lord

I was heading for a fall
And I looked up and saw the writing on the wall

In the gentle evening breeze
By the whispering shady trees
I will find my sanctuary in the Lord

No matter where I roam
I will find my way back home
I will always return to the Lord

Like a full force gale

I was lifted up again
I was lifted up again by the Lord

I was lifted up again
Lifted up
I said I was lifted up, by the Lord
Lifted up again, lifted up again
Lifted up again, by the Lord

You Make Me Feel So Free

Some people spend their time
Just running round in circles
Always chasing some exotic bird
I prefer to spend some time
Just listening for that special something
That I never ever had
I'd like a new song to sing
Another show or somewhere entirely different to be
But, baby you make me feel so free

And so I yearn for mistress calling me
That's the muse, that's the muse
But we only burn up with the passion
When there's absolutely nothing
Left to lose
I'll make it to spring
And there's no bed of roses
It's just more hard work in bad company
But, baby I want to say this, you make me feel so free

I heard them say that
You can have your cake and eat it
But all I wanted was just one free lunch
How can I eat it when the man that's next to me now
He grabbed it Lord he beat me
Beat me to the punch
How can I even talk about freedom when you know
Oh it's a sweet mystery but baby, you, you
You make me feel so free

I'm gonna lay my cards here

Right down on the table
And spin a wheel and roll the dice
And whatever way it comes out
And whatever way it turns out
Baby, you know, well that's the price
Well I'll order again there's no need to explain
I just need somewhere to dump all my negativity
But baby remember, you make me feel so free

What you say, what you say, what you say
What you say, what you say
What you say, what you say, what you say, what you say
What you say, what you say, what you say, what you say
You make me feel so free baby
Say it, say it, say it again
You make me feel so free
So doggone free

Steppin' Out Queen

Put on your lipstick
Apply your make-up
Sometimes you'll be livin'
Livin' in a dream
And then and then
Then you go stepping out queen

Then you go to a party
And you laugh loud and hearty
And you stay all night long
Oh you know you make the scene
And then you go stepping out queen

Do do do do, do do do do, do do 'n do
Stepping out
Do do do do, do do do do, do do 'n do

It's just a windfall
Just a windfall away
It keeps getting stronger every day
Baby you got to look out and say
It's a windfall away

Do do do do, do do do do, do do 'n do
Do do do do, do do do do, do do 'n do

It's just a windfall away
It's a love, it's a love, it's a love
Keeps getting stronger every day
You got to look up and say
It's a windfall away

Do do do do, do do do do, do do 'n do
It's just a windfall away
Do do do do, do do do do, do do 'n do

Well you go through the drama
And you work in the dharma
And you stand up
Stand up and wipe
Wipe your mirror clean
As you go stepping out queen

Do do do do, do do do do, do do 'n do
Stepping out
Do do do do, do do do do, do do 'n do

(Come in the garden and just look at the flowers)
This is the windfall way
(We can just sit and talk for hours and hours)
It's a love, keeps getting stronger, every day
(Come in the garden and just look at the flowers)
This is the windfall way
(We can just sit and talk for hours and hours)
It's a love, it's a love, it's a love, it's a love, it's a love,
(Come in the garden and just look at the flowers)
Come in the garden and then we'll go
(We can just sit and talk for hours and hours)
Stepping out, stepping out, stepping out

Troubadours

From the ancient sun to the old hearth stove
Sing the troubadours
From the city gates to the castle walls
Come the troubadours

On a sunlit day it was bright and clear
And the people came from far and they came from near
To hear the troubadours
Do do do do do do do do, do do do do

And the troubadours sang their songs of love
To the lady fair
She was sitting outside on her balcony
In the clear night air

It was a starry night and the moon was shining bright
And the trumpets rang and they gave a chime
For the troubadours
Do do do do do do do do, do do do do

And for every man all across the land
And from shore to shore
They come singing songs of love and chivalry
From the days of yore

Baby lift your window high do you hear that sound
It's the troubadours
As they go through town
With their freedom song, do do do do

Oh baby lift your window high do you hear that sound

It's the troubadours
With their freedom vow,
do do do, do do do do do, do, do, do, do

Baby, baby, baby lift your window high turn your lamp down
    low
Don't you know I love you so
Do you hear that sound; do you dig that sound
It's the troubadours coming through town

Satisfied

Let's go walkin' up that mountainside
Look down in the valley down below
And we survey this wondrous scene
Wait a minute
Hold that dream
Hold that dream

I want to change my name and write a book
Just like *Catcher in the Rye*
Settle down in a shady nook
Talkin' to my baby now

I'm satisfied
With my world
'Cause I made it
The way it is
Satisfied, satisfied,
Satisfied, satisfied,
Satisfied, satisfied,
Inside

Go to the mountain
Come back to the city
There's a whole lot of things
Don't look very pretty
Spiritual hunger and spiritual thirst
But you got to change it
On the inside first
To be satisfied
To be satisfied

Sometimes I think I know where it's at
Other times I'm completely in the dark
You know, baby, cause and effect
I got my karma from here right to New York

I'm satisfied
With my world
'Cause I made it
The way it is
Satisfied, satisfied
Satisfied, satisfied
Satisfied, satisfied
Inside

Sometimes I think I know how it is
Other times I'm completely in the dark
You know, baby, cause and effect
And I got my karma from here right to New York
I'm satisfied
'Cause I made it
The way it is
I'm satisfied, satisfied
Satisfied, satisfied
Satisfied, satisfied
Inside

I'm satisfied, satisfied

Wild Honey

Open your arms in the early mornin'
When the light comes shinin' through
Can't you hear my heart beat just for you
It's beating so wild, honey
And light comes shinin'

Singin' my song
And the band is playin'
And the music is tried and true
Can't you hear my heart beat just for you
It's beating so wild, honey
And light comes shinin'

I'll be waiting for you
I'll be waiting here for thee
Way up on the mountain
Where the hillside rolls down to the sea

Tell me what's real
What I feel inside
Any time of day or night will do
It's alright
Can't you hear my heart beat just for you
It's beating so wild, honey
And your light comes shining through

Tell me what's real
What I feel inside
Any time of day or night will do
It's alright
Can't you hear my heart beat just for you
It's beating so wild, honey

And the light comes shining through
And the light comes shining through
It's beating so wild, so wild, so wild, so wild, so wild, so
And the light comes shining through
And the light comes shining
And the light comes shining through

When Heart Is Open

And when heart is open
And when heart is open
You will change just like a flower slowly openin'
And when heart is open
You will change just like a flower slowly openin'
When there's no comin'
And there's no goin'

And when heart is open
You will meet your lover
You will tarry
You will tarry
In an old country

And when heart is open
You will meet your lover
When there's no comin'
And there's no goin'

Oh, hand me down my greatcoat
Oh, hand me down my greatcoat
I believe I'll go walkin' in the woods
Oh, my darlin'
Oh, hand me down my big boots
Oh, hand me down my big boots
I believe I'll go walkin' in the woods
Oh my darlin'

And she moves by the waterfall
When she moves
She moves just like a deer
Across the meadow

And when heart is open
You will change just like a flower slowly openin'
When there's no comin'
And there's no goin'
You will tarry
With your lover
And when heart is open you will meet your lover

Oh, hand me down my greatcoat
Oh, hand me down my greatcoat
I believe I'll go walkin' in the woods
Oh, my darlin
Oh, hand me down my big boots
Oh, hand me down my big boots
I believe I'll go walkin' in the woods
Oh, my darling
Oh, when she moves
She moves like a deer across the meadow

When heart is open
You will change just like a flower slowly openin'
You will change just like a flower slowly openin'

You will change just like a flower slowly openin'
When there's no comin'
When there's no comin'
And there's no goin'
You will meet
You will meet your lover
When there's no comin'
And there's no goin'
You will meet
You will meet your lover

Haunts of Ancient Peace

In haunts of ancient peace
We walk in haunts of ancient peace
At night we go to sleep and rest
In haunts of ancient peace

The love and light we seek
The words we do not need to speak
In haunts of ancient peace

We seek the Holy Grail
In haunts of ancient peace
The vision of the New Jerusalem*
Be still in haunts of ancient peace

We seek the Holy Grail
In haunts of ancient peace
And build the New Jerusalem
In haunts of ancient peace

Be still in haunts of ancient peace
Be still in haunts of ancient peace
In haunts of ancient peace
In haunts of ancient peace

* William Blake indicated the New Jerusalem was Glastonbury.

Northern Muse (Solid Ground)

And she moves on the solid ground
And she shines light all around
And she moves on the solid ground
In the County Down

And she moves on the solid earth
And she knows what her wisdom is worth
And she moves on the solid ground
In the County Down

She lifts me up, fill my cup
When I'm tired and weary, Lord
And she keeps the flame
And she give me hope
To carry on

If you see her, say hello
For she's someone that I surely know
When I was young
She made me roam from my home
In the County Down

And she moves on the solid ground
And she moves in the County Down
In the County Down

Inarticulate Speech of the Heart

Inarticulate speech, inarticulate speech of the heart
Inarticulate speech, inarticulate speech of the heart
Inarticulate speech, inarticulate speech of the heart
Inarticulate speech, inarticulate speech of the heart

I'm a soul in wonder, I'm a soul in wonder
I'm a soul in wonder, I'm a soul in wonder

Inarticulate speech, inarticulate speech of the heart
Inarticulate speech, inarticulate speech of the heart

I'm just wild about it, I can't live without it
I'm just wild about it, I can't live without it

Inarticulate speech, inarticulate speech of the heart
Inarticulate speech, inarticulate speech of the heart

I'm a soul in wonder, I'm a soul in wonder
I'm a soul in wonder, I'm a soul in wonder

I'm a soul in wonder, a soul in wonder
I'm a soul in wonder, I'm a soul in wonder
I'm a soul in wonder

A soul in wonder, I'm a soul in wonder
A soul in wonder, I'm a soul in wonder

A Sense of Wonder

I walked in my greatcoat down through the days of leaves
No before after, yes after before
We were shining our light into the days of blooming wonder
In the eternal presence, in the presence of the flame

Didn't I come to bring you a sense of wonder?
Didn't I come to lift your fiery vision bright?
Didn't I come to bring you a sense of wonder in the flame?

On and on and on we kept singing our song
Through Newtownards and Comber, Gransha and the
    Ballystockart Road
With Spike and Boffyflow, I said I would describe the leaves
    for Samuel and Felicity
Rich, red, browny, half burnt orange and green

Didn't I come to bring you a sense of wonder?
Didn't I come to lift your fiery vision bright?
Didn't I come to bring you a sense of wonder in the flame?

It's easy to describe the leaves in autumn
And it's oh so easy in the spring
But down through January and February
It's a very different thing

On and on and on, through the winter of our discontent
When the wind blows up the collar and the ears are
    frostbitten too
I said I could describe the leaves for Samuel and what it
    means to you and me
You may call my love Sophia, but I call my love Philosophy

Didn't I come to bring you a sense of wonder?
Didn't I come to lift your fiery vision bright?
Didn't I come to bring you a sense of wonder in the flame?

Didn't I, didn't I come to bring you a sense of wonder?
Didn't I come to lift your fiery vision bright?
Didn't I come to bring you a sense of wonder in the flame?

In the flame child
A sense of wonder in the flame
In the flame child

Wee Alfie at the
Castle Picture house on the Castlereagh Road
Whistling on the corner next door where
He kept Johnny Mack Brown's horse
'O Solo Mio' by McGimsey
And the man who played the saw
Outside the City Hall
Pastie suppers down at Davy's Chipper,
Gravy rings, Wagon Wheels
Barmbracks, Snowballs

A sense of wonder
A sense of wonder
A sense of wonder

On and on and on
And on and on and on

And after the days of leaves
And after the days of leaves

Oh the Warm Feeling

Oh the warm feeling
As we sat beside the sea
Oh the warm feeling
As I sat by you

Like a child within the kingdom
As we sat beside the sea
Oh the warm feeling
As I sat by you

And it filled me with devotion
And it made me plainly see
And it healed all my emotions
As I sat by you

As we sat inside the sunshine
As we sat beside the sea
Oh the warm feeling
As I sat by you

And it filled me with religion
And it gave great comfort to me
Oh the warm feeling
As I sat by you

Oh the warm feeling
As we sat beside the sea
Oh the warm feeling
As I sat by you

A Town Called Paradise

Copycats ripped off my songs
Copycats ripped off my words
Copycats ripped off my melody
It doesn't matter what they say
It doesn't matter what they do
All that matters is
My relationship to you

Gonna take you out
Get you in my car
We're goin' go for a long, long, long drive
We're goin' down
To a town called Paradise
Down where we can be free
We're gonna drink that wine
We're gonna jump for joy
In a town called Paradise

We're going up the mountainside
Child you can look for miles
And see the vision in the West
We're gonna swing round and look north
To south, east and west
And go round in a circle too

And we're gonna start dancing
Like we've never danced before
I'm gonna take you in my arms
I'm gonna squeeze you tight
Say everything will be alright
We're gonna get that squealing feeling

Gonna take you down
Baby to a town called Paradise
Down where we can be free
It doesn't matter what they say
It doesn't matter what they do
All that matters is my relationship to you
We're gonna ride all night long
All along the ancient highway
Gonna be there when the morning comes

By the river we will linger
As we drive down, down to be free
Paradise when we're dancing
Paradise in my Imagination too
Paradise with my Willpower
Paradise

Queen of the Slipstream

You're the queen of the slipstream
With eyes that shine
You have crossed many waters to here
You have drank of the fountain of innocence
And experienced the long, cold wintry years

There's a dream where the contents are visible
Where the poetic champions compose
Will you breathe not a word of this secrecy
And will you still be my special rose?

Going away far across the sea
But I'll be back for you
I will tell you everything I know
Tell me everything that's true

Will the blush still remain on your cheeks my love?
Is the light always seen in your head?
Gold and silver they placed at your feet my dear
But I know you chose me instead

Going away far across the sea
But I'll be back for you
I will tell you everything I know
Tell me everything that's true

You're the queen of the slipstream
I love you so
You have crossed many waters to be here
And you drank at the fountain of innocence
An experience you know very well

You're the queen
Queen of the slipstream
The queen of the slipstream
See you slipping and sliding in the snow
Queen of the slipstream
You come running to me
You come running to me
Queen of the slipstream

Give Me My Rapture

There are strange things happening every day
I hear music up above my head
Fill me up with your wonder
Give me my rapture today

Let me contemplate the presence so divine
Let me sing all day and never get tired
Fill me up from your loving cup
Give me my rapture today

Won't you guide me through the dark night of the soul
That I may better understand your way?
Let me be just worthy to receive
All the blessings from the Lord into my life

Give me my rapture today
Give me my rapture today
Love fill me up
From your loving cup
Give me my rapture today

Let me purify my thoughts and words and deeds
That I may be a vehicle for thee
Let me hold to the truth I know in the darkest hour
Let me sing in the glory of the Lord

Give me my rapture today
Give me my rapture today
Give me my rapture today

Contacting My Angel

Contacting my angel, contacting my angel
She's the one, she's the one that satisfies
Contacting my angel she's the one that satisfies
She's the one that I adore

Got a telepathic message from my baby
In a little village through the fog
Here comes my baby, I can tell, I can tell
By the way she walks
Said I've been on a journey up the mountainside
And I drank the water from the stream
It was pure
Pure water and it healed me

I met a presence on the mountainside
And he looked so radiant and he was the
Youth of eternal summers
Like a sweet bird of youth in my soul
In my soul, in my soul, in my soul
In my soul, in my soul, in my soul

I'd Love to Write Another Song

I'd love to write another song
But nothing seems to come
I'd love to write another song
To carry me along
Make some money, pay the bills
Keep me busy too
I'd love to write another love song

I'd love to write another song
I'm searching everywhere
Though I look for inspiration
Sometimes it's just not there
I have to work, I have to play
I have to get in step
If I could write another love song
I know it sure would help

I'd love to write another song
Baby especially for you
I'd love to write another song
And feel things bright and new
In poetry I'd carve it well
I'd even make it rhyme
I'd love to write another song
Just to get some peace of mind

I'd love to write another song
To get some peace of mind

I'd love to write another song
Baby for some peace of mind

I'm Tired Joey Boy

I'm tired Joey boy
While you're out with the sheep
My life is so troubled
That I can't go to sleep
I would walk myself out
But the streets are so dark
I shall wait till the morning
And walk in the park

This life is so simple
When one is at home
And I'm never complaining
When there's work to be done
Oh I'm tired Joey boy of the makings of men
I would like to be cheerful again

Ambition will take you and ride you too far and
Conservatism bring you to boredom once more

Sit down by the river
And watch the stream flow
Recall all the dreams
That you once used to know
The things you've forgotten
That took you away
To pastures not greener but meaner

Love of the simple is all that I need
I've no time for schism or lovers of greed
Go up to the mountain, go up to the glen
When silence will touch you
And heartbreak will mend

Daring Night

In the daring night
When all the stars are shining bright
Squeeze me don't leave me
In the daring night
Galactic swirl in the firmament tonight
Oh with the lord of the dance
With the lord of the dance
In the daring night

I see Orion and the Hunters
Standing by the light of the moon
In the daring night
In the daring night

And the heart and the soul
As we look up in awe and wonder at the heavens
Oh and we go with the lord of the dance
With the lord of the dance
With the lord of the dance
In the daring night

In the daring night
When all the stars are shining bright
Oh baby squeeze me don't leave me
In the daring night

In the firmament we move
We move, we move and we live
And we have our being
Squeeze me don't leave, leave me
In the daring night

In the firmament we move and galactic swirl
And we live and we breathe and we have our being
Baby in the daring night
Darling squeeze me, squeeze me
Don't ever leave me
In the daring night
When all the stars are shining bright

And don't let go, and don't let go
Don't let go, don't let go
In the daring night
And we move and we move, and we move and we move
And we move and we move and we move
Baby don't let go
In the daring night

In the daring night
When all the stars are shining bright
Baby squeeze me don't leave me
In the daring night

Capture it all
With the lord of the dance
Oh with the lord of the dance
In the daring night
With the lord of the dance
With the lord of the dance
And the great goddess of the eternal wisdom
Standing by the light of the moon
In the daring night

And the bodies move
And we sweat and have our being
Baby don't leave me
In the daring night

In the daring night
When all the stars are shining bright
Squeeze me don't leave me
Baby in the daring night
Baby in the daring night
In the daring night

Squeeze me don't leave me
In the daring night
In the daring night
In the daring night
And don't let go
Don't let go
Don't let go

Real Real Gone

Real, real gone
I got hit by a bow and arrow
Got me down to the very marrow
And I'm real, real gone

Real, real gone
I can't stand up by myself
Don't you know I need your help?
And I'm real, real gone

Some people say you can make it on your own
Oh you can make it if you try
I know better now you can't stand up alone
Oh baby that is why

I'm real, real gone
I can't stand up by myself
Don't you know I need your help?
You're a friend of mine
And I'm real, real gone

And Sam Cooke is on the radio
And the night is filled with space
And your fingertips touch my face
You're a friend of mine
And I'm real, real gone

I'm real gone
Oh lord I got hit by a bow and arrow
Got me down to the very marrow
You're a friend of mine

And I'm real, real gone
And I'm real, real gone
I'm real gone

Wilson Pickett said:
'In the midnight hour, that's
When my love comes tumbling down'

Solomon Burke said:
'If you need me, why don't you call me?'

James Brown said:
'When you're tired of what you got, try me'

Gene Chandler said:
'There's a rainbow in my soul'

Enlightenment

Chop that wood
Carry water
What's the sound of one hand clapping?
Enlightenment, don't know what it is

Every second, every minute
It keeps changing to something different

Enlightenment, don't know what it is
Enlightenment, don't know what it is
It says it's non-attachment, non-attachment, non-attachment

I'm in the here and now, and I'm meditating
And still I'm suffering but that's my problem
Enlightenment, don't know what it is

Wake up

Enlightenment says the world is nothing
Nothing but a dream
Everything's an illusion and nothing is real

Good or bad baby
You can change it any way you want
You can rearrange it
Enlightenment, don't know what it is

Chop that wood
And carry water
What's the sound of one hand clapping?
Enlightenment, don't know what it is

All around baby, you can see
You're making your own reality, every day because
Enlightenment, don't know what it is

One more time

Enlightenment, don't know what it is
It's up to you
Enlightenment, don't know what it is
It's up to you every day
Enlightenment, don't know what it is
It's always up to you
Enlightenment, don't know what it is
It's up to you, the way you think

Youth of 1000 Summers

He's the youth of a thousand summers
He's the youth of a thousand summers
Like a sweet bird of youth
Like a sweet bird of youth
In my soul, in my soul, in my soul
In my soul, in my soul, in my soul

And he looks so radiant
And he shines like the sun
And he looks so radiant
And he lights up the world

He's the youth of a thousand summers
He's the youth of a thousand summers
Like a sweet bird of youth
Like a sweet bird of youth
In my soul, in my soul, in my soul
In my soul, in my soul, in my soul

In my soul, in my soul, in my soul
In my soul, in my soul, in my soul

He's the king of the mountain
And the clear crystal fountain
He's the saint of the river
He's the ancient of days

He's the youth of a thousand summers
He's the youth of a thousand summers
Like a sweet bird of youth
Like a sweet bird of youth

In my soul, in my soul, in my soul
In my soul, in my soul, in my soul

And he makes you go skipping
And he makes you go dancing
And he gets you in rhythm
And he moves you in song

He's the youth of a thousand summers
He's the youth of a thousand summers
Like a sweet bird of youth
Like a sweet bird of youth
In my soul, in my soul, in my soul
In my soul, in my soul, in my soul
In my soul, in my soul, in my soul
In my soul, in my soul, in my soul

And a sweet bird of youth
In my soul

Professional Jealousy

Professional jealousy can bring down a nation
And personal invasion can ruin a man
Not even his family will understand what's happening
The price that he's paying or even the pain

Professional jealousy started a rumour
And then it extended to be more abuse
What started out as just black propaganda
Was one day seen to be believed as truth

They say the truth is stranger than fiction
But a lie is more deadly than sin
It can make a man very bitter and angry
When he thinks that there's someone, is going to win

Professional jealousy makes others crazy
They think you've got something that they don't have
What they don't understand is it's not that easy
To cover the miles and be where you are

They say that the truth is stranger than fiction
But a lie is more deadly than sin
It can make men bitter, bitter and angry
When they think that someone else is going to win

Professional jealousy makes other people crazy
When they think you've got something that they don't
    have
What they don't understand is it's just not easy
To cover it all and stand where you stand

Professional jealousy makes no exception
It can happen to anyone at any time
The only requirement is knowing what's needed
And then delivering what's needed on time

The only requirement is to know what is needed
In doing the best you know how, deliver on time
The only requirement is to know what is needed
Be best at delivering the product on time

I'm Not Feeling It Anymore

Have to get back, have to get back to base
I need to talk to somebody I can trust
Too many cooks are tryin' to spoil the broth
I can't feel it in my throat, that's all she wrote

I'm not feeling it no more, I'm not feeling it anymore
Not feelin' it no more, not feelin' it anymore

When I was high at the party, everything looked good
I was seein' through rose-coloured glasses
Not seein' the wood for the trees
I started out in normal operation
But I just ended up in doubt
All my drinking buddies, they locked me out

I'm not feelin' it no more, I'm not feelin' it anymore
Not feelin' it no more, I'm tryin' to give you the score

You see me up there baby, I'm on the screen
But I know better now, it's so unreal
If this is success, then something's awful wrong
'Cause I bought the dream and I had to play along

I'm not feelin' it no more, I'm not feelin' it anymore
I'm tryin' to give you the score, I'm not feelin' it no more

We all know that money don't buy you love
You just get a job and somewhere to live
You have to look for happiness within yourself
And don't go chasin' thinkin' that it is somewhere else

I'm not feelin' it no more, I'm not feelin' it anymore
Baby I'm tryin' to give you the score
I'm not feelin' it no more

I was pretending all the time
I was givin' everybody what they wanted
And I lost my peace of mind
And all I ever wanted was simply just to be me
All you ever need is the truth
And the truth will set you free

I'm not feelin' it no more, I'm not feelin' it anymore
I'm tryin' to give you the score, just like I did before
I'm not feelin' it no more, I'm not feelin' it anymore
I'm not feelin' it no more
Baby I'm just trying to give you the score
I'm not feelin' it no more, not feelin' it anymore
Not feelin' it no more
Not feelin' it no more

Some Peace of Mind

You see me on the street, well you guess I'm doing fine
Oh but it's fantasy baby, almost all the time
I've got to get away, by myself
Oh the way it's going, soon be needing help
'Cause I'm just a man, doing the best I can
Don't you understand, I just want some peace of mind

You see me on the stage, doing my job
I learn to do it well, keep on singing the song
But sometimes it gets so lonely out there
When you're on the road and you're going nowhere
Because I'm just a man, oh I ain't got no plans
Don't you understand, I'm just trying to find some peace of
    mind

I have to stand in line, baby when I'm in the queue
I got to do it all, just the same as you
Got my doubts about it, oh but I try
Oh I make it work with tears in my eyes
Because I'm just a man, only trying to do the best I can
Don't you understand, I want some peace of mind

Oh I'm just a man, baby I ain't got no plan
Oh don't you understand, got to get some peace of mind
Oh got to get, got to get some peace of mind
Oh got to get, got to get some peace of mind
Got to get, get some peace of mind
Get me some, get me some, some peace of mind
Get me some, get me some, peace of mind

Village Idiot

Did you see the lad on the corner?
He was standing drinking wine
Wears his overcoat in the summer
And short sleeves in the wintertime

Takes his holidays down at the bookies
Well he knows how to pick a horse
Village tramping round the countryside
He wears a smile, but he doesn't say much

Village idiot, he's complicated
Village idiot, simple mind
Village idiot, he does know something
But he's just not saying

Don't you know he's onto something?
You can see it, you can see it in his eyes
Sometimes he looks so happy
As he goes strolling by

Oh village idiot, he's complicated
Village idiot, he's got a simple mind
Village idiot, must know something
But he's just not saying

Well you all know he's onto something
You can see it in his eyes
Sometimes he looks so happy
When he goes walking by
Sometimes he looks so happy
When he goes walking by

Sometimes he looks so happy
When he goes walking by

Carrying a Torch

I'm carryin' a torch for you
I'm carryin' a torch
You know how much it costs
To keep carryin' a torch

Flame of love it burns so bright
That is my desire
Keep on liftin' me, liftin' me up
Higher and higher

You're the keeper of the flame
And you burn so bright
Baby why don't we re-connect
Move into the light

I've been going to and fro on this
And I'm still carryin' a torch
You must know how much it's worth
When I'm carryin' a torch

Baby you're the keeper of the flame
And you burn so bright
Why, why, why, why, why, why don't we re-connect
And move on further, into the light

I've been calling you on the phone
'Cause I'm carryin' a torch
I can do it all on my own
'Cause I'm carryin' a torch

I'm carryin' a torch for you, baby

I'm carryin' a torch
You know how much it's worth
Because I'm carryin' a torch

I'm carryin' a torch for you, baby
I'm carryin' a torch
You know how much it's worth
Because I'm carryin' a torch

Pagan Streams

And we walked the pagan streams
And searched for white horses on surrounding hills
We lived where dusk had meaning
And repaired to quiet sleep, where noise abated
In touch with the silence
On Honey Street, on Honey Street

What happened to a sense of wonder?
On yonder hillside, getting dim
Why didn't they leave us, alone?
Why couldn't we just be ourselves?
We could dream, and keep bees
And live on Honey Street

And we walked the pagan streams
In meditation and contemplation
And we didn't need anybody, or anything then
No concepts, being free
And I wanna climb that hillside again, with you
One more time

As the great, great, great, great, great, great, great
Being watches over
And we repair, repair, repair, shhh, repair, shhh, we repair
To Honey Street, to Honey Street

I Need Your Kind of Loving

Well my baby's gone, so's summer
And it brings on a cool night breeze
And I wish we could go walking
By the river, by the shady trees
By the river with the shady trees

Well I love you in the wintertime
Baby when the snow is on the ground
Well I love you in the autumn most of all
When the leaves come tumbling down
When the leaves come tumbling down

Baby I need your kind of loving
For to last my whole life through
Baby I need your kind of loving
You know nobody else will do
You know that nobody else will do

Well I love you in the springtime
When the rippling streams begin to flow
And the weather starts to get a bit warmer
And the grass begins to grow
And the green, green, grass begins to grow

Baby I need your kind of loving
For to last my whole life through
Baby I need your kind of loving
You know that nobody else will do
You know that nobody else will do

Baby I need your kind of loving

For to last my whole life through
Baby I need your kind of loving
You know nobody else will do
You know nobody else will do

Need your kind of loving
Operator, operator
Put me through to my baby now
Operator, put me through to my baby now
To my baby now, to my baby now

Big Time Operators

Well, they told me to come on over
I made my way to New York
And they tried to have me deported
Stop me from getting work
Blacklisted me all over
They were vicious and they were mean
They were big time operators
Baby, on the music business scene

Oh, they looked like politicians
But underneath they were thugs
And they spread malicious rumours
Threatened to have me busted for drugs
They had nothing on me
Oh man, I was really clean
But they were big time operators
On the music business scene

They put a bug in my apartment
To listen in on my calls
I was looking for some motivation
I couldn't find any, any motivation at all
They were very desperate people
Riding in long black limousines
But they were big time operators
On the music business scene

They were glorified by the media
They were heroes who had names
They said that they would bury me
If I didn't play their game

They said I didn't know the score
And that I was young and green
They were big time operators
On the music business scene

Tried to hold me to a phoney contract
I said I didn't agree
Had to get out of their clutches
Had to go underground you see
Now I'm living in another country
But I know exactly just where I've been
Stay away from big time operators
Baby, on the music business scene

Well, baby, big time operators
On the music business scene
Oh baby, big time operators
On the music business scene
Well, full of names and places
Baby, you know who I mean

Perfect Fit

Now baby just lately you've been holding back too much
Your looks and my language, this could be the perfect touch
What you are asking fits with everything on my list
This could be the perfect fit

Tell me that it's madness to want something quite like this
But they don't understand the magic that I can't resist
Oh and wouldn't it be so tragic if everything just went amiss
And this could be the perfect fit

They say no one is perfect, some people might take the piss
And we say we're just friends, come on, tell me what's wrong
    with this
But I say keep it simple, well we haven't even started yet
And this could be the perfect fit

See that dress you're wearing baby, said it suits you right
    down to the ground
Tell me where in the world a better loving woman can be
    found
Well I've searched high and low now and from where you
    and I sit
And this could be the perfect fit

See that dress you're wearing, suits you right down to the
    ground
Tell me where in the world a better loving woman can be
    found
And I've searched high and low now and from where you
    and I sit
Baby, this could be the perfect fit

Baby, this could be the perfect fit
Come on baby, this could be the perfect fit

Fit, fit, fit, fit, fit, fit, fit, fit, say again
This could be the perfect fit
Fit, fit, fit, fit, fit, fit, fit, fit, fit
This could be the perfect fit

Ancient Highway

There's a small cafe on the outskirts of town
I'll be there when the sun goes down
Where the roadside bends
And it twists and turns
Every new generation
And I'll be praying to my Higher Self
Don't let me down, keep my feet on the ground

There's a roadside jam playin' on the edge of the town
In a town called Paradise near the ancient highway
When the train whistle blows
All the sadness that Hank Williams knows
And the river flows
Call them pagan streams and it spins and it turns
In a factory in a street called Bread in East Belfast
Where Georgie knows best
What it's like to be Daniel in the lion's den
Got so many friends only most of the time

When the grass is high and the rabbit runs
Though it's talkin' to you and I
And every new generation comes to pay
The dues of the organ grinder jam
And the Grinder's Switch of the sacrifice
Everybody made to be rational with understanding
And I'll be praying to my higher self
Oh, don't let me down, keep my feet on the ground

What about all the people living in the nightmare hurt
That won't go away no matter how hard they try
They've got to pay time and time again, time and time again

I'll be praying to my higher self
And I'll be standin' there, where the boats go by
When the sun is sinking way over the hill
On a Friday evening when the sun goes down
On the outskirts of town, I wanna slip away
I wanna slip away, got to get away
And I'll be praying to my higher self
Don't let me down, keep my feet on the ground, don't let me
      down

You'll be cryin' again, you'll be cryin' again, you'll be cryin'
      again
By the same wipe the teardrops from your eyes
Have to slip away in the evening when the sun goes down
Over the hill, with a sense of wonder
Everything gonna be right on a Friday evening
All the cars go by all along down
The ancient highway
And I'll be praying, I'll be praying to my higher self
Don't let me down, keep my feet, keep my feet on the ground
Keep my feet on the ground

Travelling like a stranger in the night, all along the ancient
      highway
Got you in my sights, got you on my mind
I'll be praying in the evening when the sun goes down
Over the mountain, got to get you right in my sight
As the beams from the cars from the overpass
On the ancient highway shine just like diamonds in the night
Like diamonds in the night
I'll be praying to my Higher Self, to my Higher Self
Don't let me down, don't let me down

And you'll be standing there, where the boats go by
Where the boats go by on a Friday evening

Shining your light, shining your light on a Friday evening
Got to slip away, got to slip away down that ancient highway
In a town called Paradise, in a town, in a town
All along, all along that road, all along that road,
All along that road with the trancelike vision
Trancelike vision, trancelike vision
Trancelike vision on my mind

I'll be praying to my higher self, don't let me down, don't let
    me down
Keep my feet on the ground, keep my feet on the ground,
Keep my feet on the ground
Keep my feet on the ground

Friday evening got to slip away
Watching the view from a car from the overpass
And we're driving down that ancient road
Shining like diamonds in the night, oh diamonds in the night
All along the ancient highway
Got you in my sight, got you in my mind
Got you in my arms and I'm praying, and I'm gonna pray
I'm gonna pray, to my Higher Self, ah don't let me down
Don't let me down, give me the fire, give me the fire

In the Afternoon

The light is fading in the afternoon
Won't you see me baby in my room
There's something that I wanna say to you
Tell me baby am I getting through?
Wanna make, wanna make, wanna make, wanna make
Love to you
Wanna make, wanna make, wanna make, wanna make
Love to you
Wanna make, wanna make, wanna make, wanna make
Love to you
In the afternoon, in the afternoon

The light is fading from across the way
I see you coming baby every day
I see you running, running from across the field
And I wanna know if you feel the same as me
'Cause I wanna make, wanna make, wanna make, wanna
    make
Love to you
Wanna make, wanna make, wanna make, wanna make
Love to you
Wanna make, wanna make, wanna make, wanna make
Love to you
In the afternoon, in the afternoon

The wind is howling baby outside the shack
Train whistle blowin' from across the track
Get on my wavelength, and you set me free
I just wanna be everything you want me to be
Wanna make, wanna make, wanna make, wanna make
Love to you

Wanna make, wanna make, wanna make, wanna make
Love to you
Wanna make, wanna make, wanna make, wanna make
Love to you
In the afternoon, in the afternoon

The moon is sinking way across the trees
I can see my baby but she can't see me
I've got a longing deep within my soul
I have to take it there and let it roll
Wanna make, wanna make, wanna make, wanna make,
    wanna make
Love to you
Wanna make, wanna make, wanna make, wanna make,
Love to you
Wanna make, wanna make, wanna make, wanna make,
Love to you
In the afternoon, make love in the afternoon
Make love in the afternoon

Let it roll
You got me reelin' and a-rockin' and rollin' again
Let it roll
You got me reelin' and a rockin' and rollin' and rollin' again
Oh, I'm rollin' and tumblin', and I'm rollin' and tumblin'
And I'm talkin' all outta my mind baby

Let it roll
You got me reelin' and a-rockin'
And I'm talkin' all outta my mind

I'm talkin' all outta my mind
Make love in the afternoon
Make love in the afternoon
Make love in the afternoon

Rough God Goes Riding

Oh the mud-splattered victims
Have to pay out all along the ancient highway
Torn between half-truth and victimisation
Fighting back with counter attacks

It's when that rough god goes riding
When the rough god goes gliding
When that rough god goes riding
Riding on in

I was flabbergasted by the headlines
People in glasshouses throwing stones
Gaping wounds that will never heal
Now they're moaning like a dog in a manger

It's when that rough god goes riding
When that rough god goes gliding
There'll be nobody hiding
When that rough god comes riding on in

And it's a matter of survival
When you're born with your back against the wall
Won't somebody hand me a bible
Won't you give me that number to call?

When that rough god goes riding
And then that rough god goes gliding
There'll be nobody hiding
When that rough god goes riding on in, riding on in

When that rough god goes riding
When that rough god goes gliding
There'll be nobody hiding
When that rough god goes riding on in
Riding on in

There'll be no more heroes
They'll be reduced to zero
When that rough god goes riding
Riding on in
Riding on in
Riding on in
Riding on in

This Weight

This weight is weighing on my heart
This weight is tearing us apart
This weight is weighing on my soul
And it just won't leave me alone

You know I'm talking about this weight
You know I'm talking about this weight

In the neighbourhood people watching me
Got to move to protect my sanity
Anonymity is all I want you see
You may think it's mediocrity, but

You know I'm talking about this weight
You know I'm talking about this weight

And the Hollywood ain't no good
I would rather be like Robin Hood
If I could only lose this

You know I'm talking about this weight
You know I'm talking about this weight

And this Hollywood ain't no good
I would rather be just like Robin Hood
If I could only lose this

You know I'm talking about this weight
You know I'm talking about this weight

In the very first it was rock 'n' roll
Set me free in body and soul
But this weight is just bringing me down
It's never satisfied every time I go to town
You know I'm talking about this weight

You know I'm talking about this weight
You know I'm talking about this weight
You know I'm talking about this weight

Waiting Game

On a golden autumn day returning
Where each moment never is the same
And pure joy it sometimes comes with patience
When I'm waiting on, waiting game
When I'm waiting on, waiting game

There must be reason for all this inaction
Does it mean that everything must change?
Sometimes I'm looking for perfection
When I'm waiting on, waiting game
When I'm waiting on, waiting game

I am the observer who is observing
I am the brother of the snake
I am the serpent filled with venom
The god of love and the god of hate

There is a presence deep within you
Sometimes they call it higher flame
And the leaves come tumbling down, remember
I'll be waiting on, waiting game
I'll be waiting on, waiting game

I am the observer who is observing
I am the brother of the snake
I am the serpent filled with venom
The god of love and the god of hate

There is a presence deep within you
Some people call it higher power in flame
When the leaves come tumbling down, remember

I'll be waiting on, waiting game
I'll be waiting on, waiting game

Waiting on the waiting game
Waiting on,
Waiting on,
Then I'll come, the waiting game

Piper at the Gates of Dawn

The coolness of the riverbank, and the whispering of the
    reeds
Daybreak is not so very far away

Enchanted and spellbound, in the silence they lingered
And rowed the boat as the light grew steadily strong
And the birds were silent, as they listened for the heavenly
    music
And the river played the song

The Wind in the Willows and the Piper at the Gates of Dawn
The Wind in the Willows and the Piper at the Gates of Dawn

The song dream happened and the cloven hoofed piper
Played in that holy ground where they felt the awe and
    wonder
And they all were unafraid of the great god Pan

And the Wind in the Willows and the Piper at the Gates of
    Dawn
The Wind in the Willows and the Piper at the Gates of Dawn

When the vision vanished they heard a choir of birds singing
In the heavenly silence between the trance and the reeds
And they stood upon the lawn and listened to the silence

Of the Wind in the Willows and the Piper at the Gates of
    Dawn
The Wind in the Willows and the Piper at the Gates of Dawn
The Wind in the Willows and the Piper at the Gates of Dawn

It's the Wind in the Willows and the Piper at the Gates of
   Dawn
The Wind in the Willows and the Piper at the Gates of Dawn
The Wind in the Willows and the Piper at the Gates of Dawn

It Once Was My Life

There were people on the sidewalks
Strolling down the avenues
They were sitting outside in cafes
We were looking for the muse
Well I was locked in by the system
Where no freedom is the rule
Now I spend all my time just trying
To make it understood

It once was my life, that's what everybody said
All the things I used to do and the people that were friends
I've got to make it mean something at the end of the day
It once was my life, they can't take that away

Trials and tribulations and stupidity still rules
Sometimes it looks like I'm on a ship of fools

It once was my life, when my message was just the street
Then it became something else, and now I'm incomplete
I'm just trying to get back to when
Can somebody please shed some light?
It used to be my life, it used to be uptight

Trials and tribulations and stupidity still rules
Some days it just feels like I'm on a ship of fools

I'm back here on the boards, I can hear the engines roar
Everybody's got to pay, some people got to pay more
Well you can tell the people anything
Spoon feed them anything you like
It used to be so simple, it used to be my life

Now everything is so complicated, just to speak or use the
 phone
Some people try to use me, just 'cause they don't have their
 own
Don't know who's round the corner, trying to sell me some
 more tripe
It used to be my life, it used to be my life
It used to be my life, it used to be my life

The Healing Game

Here I am again
Back on the corner again
Back where I belong
Where I've always been
Everything the same
It don't ever change
I'm back on the corner again
In the healing game

Down those ancient streets
Down those ancient roads
Where nobody knows
Where nobody goes
I'm back on the corner again
Where I've always been
Never been away
From the healing game

Where the choirboys sing
Where I've always been
Sing the song with soul
Baby don't you know
We can let it roll
On the saxophone
Back street jellyroll
In the healing game

Where the homeboys sing
Sing their songs of praise
'Bout their golden days
In the healing game

Sing it out loud
Sing it in your name
Sing it like you're proud
Sing the healing game
Sing it out loud
Sing it in your name
Sing it like you're proud
Sing the healing game

Sing the healing game
Sing the healing game
Sing it in your name
Sing the healing game

Wonderful Remark

How can you stand the silence
That pervades when we all cry?
How can you watch the violence
That erupts before your eyes?

You can't even grab a hold on
When we're hanging oh so loose
You don't even listen to us
When we talk it ain't no use

Leave your thoughtlessness behind you
Then you may begin to understand
Cleave the emptiness around you
With the waving of your hand

That was a wonderful remark
I had my eyes closed in the dark
I sighed a million sighs
I told a million lies to myself, to myself

Now, how can we listen to you
When we know that your talk is cheap?
How can we never question
Why we give more and you keep?

How can your empty laughter
Fill a room like ours with joy?
When you're only playing with us
Like a child does with a toy

How can we ever feel the freedom

Or the flame lit by the spark?
How can we ever come out even
When reality is stark?

That was a wonderful remark
I had my eyes closed in the dark
I sighed a million sighs
I told a million lies to myself, to myself

Listen, how can you tell us something
Just to keep us hanging on
Something that just don't mean nothin'
When we see you, you are gone

Clinging to some other rainbow
While we're standing waiting outside in the cold
Telling us the same sad story
Knowing time is growing old

Touch your world up with some colour
Dream you're swinging on a star
Taste it first then add some flavour
Now you know just who you are

That was a wonderful remark
I had my eyes closed in the dark
I sighed a million sighs
I told a million lies to myself, to myself

Wonderful remark
And that, that was a wonderful remark
I had my eyes closed in the dark
I sighed a million sighs
I told a million lies to myself, to myself

Don't Worry about Tomorrow

Don't worry about tomorrow
That ain't gonna help you none
Don't worry about tomorrow
That ain't gonna help you none
You gotta live and take each day as it comes

It may not be exactly what you're looking for
It may not be exactly what you're looking for
But what you're looking for ain't gonna come walking
Through your front hall door, oh no

So, don't worry about tomorrow
Gotta live each day as it comes
Don't worry about tomorrow
You gotta live each day as it comes
It's the only way you seem to get things done

Try for Sleep

It's four o'clock in the morning, and there's a new full moon
Shining down through the trees
But don't leave the room now, leave it in doubt
Pretend not to know what I'm talking about
I try all night long
I try, I want you to come along

I feel it when you touch me, I'm already wet
But how are you supposed to know what you get
Wake me when it's over, but don't turn on the light
Call me by name, that's alright
I try, all night long,
Ooh, I try to carry on

And, how can you go through, how can you go through
So many changes
Oh, how can you go through, how can you go through
So many changes
It's a family affair, it's a family affair
It's a family affair, it's a family affair, it's a family affair
Try for sleep, why don't you try for sleep
Why don't you try for sleep?

I'm pushin' the river, ready to roll
Oh, I can feel it in my soul
Give me the highlight and leave out the rest
You know what they told me
They said the west is best
I try, all night long, I try to get along with
Will try for sleep, ooh try for sleep
Won't you, oh won't you come along, come along

Try for sleep, try for sleep
I want you to try for sleep
I know you will try, ooh baby
Ooh baby, baby, baby, baby, baby

Drumshanbo Hustle

Lord have mercy! Feel so good
I think I'm gonna work

I was talking to the Judge, just before we left the countryside
Piece of paper in his hand, tryin' to find the way
Tryin' to rip it out, well now I've got it all around
Tore the pages up before they brought the curtain down

I remember the day, the 'Drumshanbo hustle'
When you couldn't hear a bird, it was making not a sound
They were trying to muscle in, an easy way to bring the
    money in
You were puking up your guts
When you looked at the standard contract you just signed

Prostitution on the run, 'cepting when it was soliciting
Tryin' to drain them all dry, got hung up by the rope
Magazines and books, clearly undefinable
Wiped the clean slate, and pulled the rug from underneath
    our feet

I remember the day, the 'Drumshanbo hustle'
When you couldn't hear no birds, 'cos they were making not
    a sound
They were trying to muscle in, the recording and the
    publishing
You were puking up your guts
When you read the standard contract you just signed

New York hooker by the neck, reads your Tarot cards and
    astronomy

Hey, I want to get your stars but don't know your sign
It was taking time to get the message through to it
But will hand down shake you one, and a letter five 'T' rhyme
No sign poker

Oh, remember the day, the 'Drumshanbo hustle'
Couldn't hear a bird, Lord, you couldn't hear no sound
They were trying to muscle in
On the gigs and the recording and the publishing
You were puking up your guts
When you read the standard contract you just signed

You were puking up your guts
When you read the standard contract that you signed
You were puking up your guts
When you read the standard contract you just signed

Goin' Down Geneva

Goin' down Geneva, give me a helping hand
I'm goin' down Geneva, give me a helping hand
It's not easy baby, living on the exile plan

Down on the bottom, down to my new pair of shoes
Down on the bottom, down to my new pair of shoes
I'm down by the lakeside, thinking 'bout my baby blue

Last night I played a gig in Salzburg, outside in the pouring rain
Last night I played a gig in Salzburg, outside in the pouring rain
Flew from there to Montreux and my heart was filled with pain

Look out my window, back at the way things are
Look out my window pane, back at the way things are
Just wonder how, how did things ever get this far

Vince Taylor used to live here, nobody's ever heard of him
Vince Taylor used to live here, but nobody's heard of him, ain't
    that a shame
Just who he was, just where he fits in

He was goin' down Geneva, give him a helping hand
He was goin' down Geneva, give him a helping hand
It wasn't easy living on the exile plan

Vince Taylor used to live here, nobody's even heard of him
Vince, Vince Taylor lives here, nobody's even heard of him
Just who he was, just where he fits in

Just who he was, just where he fits in

In the Midnight

In the lonely, dead of midnight
In the dimness of the twilight
By the streetlight, by the lamplight
I'll be around

In the sunlight, in the daylight
When I'm workin', on the insight
And I'm tryin' to keep my game uptight
I'll be around

In your memory, I heard this lonely, lonely music once
In your memory, it's been haunting me ever since

When I'm tryin', tryin' to come down
In my world, my room keeps spinning round
And I'm tryin' to get my feet back on the ground
You'll come around

In my memory, I heard the lonely, lonely music once
In my memory, it's been haunting me ever since

In the lonely, dead of midnight
In the dimness of the twilight
If you meet me, by the lamplight
I'll be around

When I'm tryin' for the come down
And my room keeps spinning round and round
And I'm tryin' to get my feet right back on the ground
You'll come around

When the Leaves Come Falling Down

I saw you standing with the wind and the rain in your face
And you were thinking 'bout the wisdom of the leaves and
    their grace
When the leaves come falling down
In September when the leaves, come falling down

And at night the moon is shining on a clear, cloudless sky
But when the evening shadows fall I'll be there by your side
When the leaves come falling down
In September when the leaves come falling down

Follow me down, follow me down, follow me down
To the place beside the garden and the wall
Follow me down, follow me down
To the space before the twilight and the dawn

Oh, the last time I saw Paris in the streets, in the rain
And as I walk along the boulevards with you, once again
And the leaves come falling down
In September when the leaves, leaves come falling down

Follow me down, follow me down, follow me down
To the place between the garden and the wall
Follow me down, follow me down
To the space between the twilight and the dawn

And as I'm looking at the colour of the leaves, in your hand
As we're listening to Chet Baker on the beach, in the sand
When the leaves come falling down,
Oh in September, when the leaves come falling down
Oh when the leaves come falling down

In September when the leaves come falling down

When the leaves come falling down
In September, when the leaves, leaves come falling down

When the leaves come falling down in September, in the rain
When the leaves come falling down

When the leaves come falling down in September, in the rain
When the leaves come falling down

Precious Time

Precious time is slipping away
But you're only king for a day
It doesn't matter to which God you pray
Precious time is slipping away

It doesn't matter what route you take
Sooner or later the heart's going to break
No rhyme or reason, no master plan
No Nirvana, no promised land

Because, precious time is slipping away
You know you're only king for a day
It doesn't matter to which God you pray
Precious time is slipping away

Say que sera, whatever will be
But then I keep on searching for immortality
She's so beautiful but she's going to die some day
Everything in life just passes away

Precious time is slipping away
You know she's only queen for a day
It doesn't matter to which God you pray
Precious time is slipping away

Well this world is cruel with its twists and its turns
Well the fire's still in me and the passion burns
I love her madly 'til the day I die
'Til hell freezes over and the rivers run dry

Precious time is slipping away

You know she's only queen for a day
Doesn't matter to which God you pray because
Precious time is slipping away

Precious time is slipping away
You know you're only king for a day
Doesn't matter to which God you pray
Precious time is slipping away

Precious time is slipping away
You know you're only king for a day
Doesn't matter to which God you pray because
Precious time is slipping away

Golden Autumn Day

Well I heard the bells ringing, I was thinking about winning
In this God forsaken place
When my confidence was well, then I tripped and I fell
Right flat on my face
Now I'm standing erect, and I feel like coming back
And the sun is shining gold
Put a smile on my face, get back in the human race
And get on with the show

And I'm taking in the Indian Summer
And I'm soaking it up in my mind
And I'm pretending that it's paradise
On a golden autumn day, on a golden autumn day
On a golden autumn day, on a golden autumn day
In the wee midnight hour I was parking my car
In this dimly lit town,
I was attacked by two thugs, who took me for a mug
And shoved me down on the ground
And they pulled out a knife, and I fought my way out
As they scarpered from the scene
Well this is no New York street, and there's no Bobby on the
    beat
And things just what they seem

And I'm taking in the Indian Summer
And I'm soaking it up in my mind
And I'm pretending that it's paradise
On a golden autumn day, on a golden autumn day
On a golden autumn day, on a golden autumn day

Who would think this could happen in a city like this

Among Blake's green and pleasant hills,
And we must remember as we go through September
Among these dark satanic mills
If there's such a thing as justice I could take them out and
    flog them
In the nearest green field
And it might be a lesson to the bleeders of the system
In this whole society

And I'm taking in the Indian Summer
And I'm soaking it up in my mind
And I'm pretending like it's paradise
On a golden autumn day, on a golden autumn day
On a golden autumn day, on a golden autumn day

Golden autumn day

Meet Me in the Indian Summer

Well don't you know
How much I love you
Don't you know
How much I care
It's beyond my comprehension
'Cos I love you on the square

It's not bound by any definition
It isn't written in the stars
It's not limited like Saturn
It isn't ruled by Mercury or Mars

Oh won't you meet me
In the Indian summer?
Where we'll go walking
Down by the weeping willow tree
Won't you meet me
In the Indian summer?
We'll go walking to eternity

It's not modelled by convention
It isn't worshipped like the sun
It's not likened unto any other
And it will never come undone

Well don't you know
That my world is so lonely?
Just like a freight train in the dawn
That's why I need to
Have and hold you
Just to keep me from going wrong

Oh won't you meet me
In the Indian summer?
We'll go walking
By the weeping willow tree
Won't you meet me Lord
In the Indian summer?

We'll go walking to eternity

Won't you meet me
In the Indian summer?
Well before
Those chilly winds do blow
Won't you meet me

In the Indian summer?
Take me way back
To what I know

Oh won't you meet me
In the Indian summer?
We'll go walking
By the weeping willow tree
Oh won't you meet me
In the Indian summer?
We'll go walking to eternity

Whatever Happened to PJ Proby?

Whatever happened to PJ Proby?
Wonder can you fix it Jim
Where the hell do you think is Scott Walker?
My memory's getting so dim

Don't have no frame of reference no more
Not even Screaming Lord Sutch
Without him now there's no Raving Loony Party
Nowadays I guess there's not much

To relate to anymore
Unless you wanna be mediocre
Ain't nothing new under the sun
And the moon and the stars, now chum

I'm making my way down the highway
Still got a monkey on my back
Facing head on and doing it my way
Please can you cut me some slack?

Nothing to relate to anymore
Unless you want to be mediocre
Ain't nothing new under the sun
And the moon and the stars, now chum

Still making my way down the highway
Still got a monkey on my back
Facing head on and doing it my way
Please can you cut me some slack?

All the cards fell so many rounds
Down the road a piece Jack
I saw a bus coming and I had to get on it
I'm still trying to find my way back

Whatever happened to all those dreams a while ago?
Whatever happened way across the sea?
Whatever happened to the way it's supposed to happen?
And whatever happened to me?

The Beauty of the Days Gone By

When I recall just how it felt
When I went walking down by the lake
My soul was free, my heart awake
When I walked down into the town

The mountain air was fresh and clear
The sun was up behind the hill
It felt so good to be alive
On that morning in spring

I want to sing this song for you
I want to lift your spirits high
And in my soul I want to feel
The beauty of the days gone by

The beauty of the days gone by
It brings a longing to my soul
To contemplate my own true self
And keep me young as I grow old

The beauty of the days gone by
The music that we used to play
So lift your glass and raise it high
To the beauty of the days gone by

I'll sing it from the mountain top
Down to the valley down below
Because my cup doth overflow
With the beauty of the days gone by

The mountain glen

Where we used to roam
The gardens there
By the railroad track
Oh my memory it does not lie
Of the beauty of the days gone by

The beauty of the days gone by
It brings a longing to my soul
To contemplate my own true self
And keep me young as I grow old

And keep me young as I grow old
And keep me young as I grow old
And keep me young as I grow old

Man Has to Struggle

Man makes his money and they call him rich
Deep down inside he knows that life's still a bitch
Man tries to keep things but they're taken away
Man has to struggle all the live long day

Man has to sweat and toil his life filled with trouble
Man got to step and fetch it on the double
Man has to work so hard to make it all pay
Man has to struggle all the live long day

Man keeps on moving 'cos he can't keep still
Man has to set his goals and climb up the hill
Man sees the mountains and the deep blue sky
Man has to struggle till the day that he die

Well yes siree Bob, them there's the breaks
That's how it is my friend don't make no mistake

Man has to take some action all of the time
Man by his nature's never satisfied
Man just can't vegetate no matter what they say
Man has to make it all the live long day

Man has to create karma that's the way that it is
Man has to keep on going way beyond his will
Man has to keep on being 'cos there's nothing else
And man just always has to go for himself

Take all the gurus when they meditate
Transcend the mundane into some altered state
You just might get there, but you'll have to pay

Man's got to struggle all the live long day

Well yes siree now Bob, them there's the breaks
That's how it is my friend don't make no mistake

Man has to watch the weather and the food that he eats
Man has to keep fit 'else he's prone to disease
No matter what he does there's stress every which-a-way
Man has to struggle all the live long day

Man is in conflict with his natural self
Man has to suppress his own desires and instincts
Man has to work so hard to keep them at bay
Man has to struggle all the live long day

Man was told that he was born in original sin
By people long ago that were conning him
Man is so out of touch he can't trust himself
But man's still got to win by cunning and stealth

Fast Train

Well you've been on a fast train and it's going off the rails
And you can't come back can't come back together again
And you start breaking down
In the pouring rain
When you've been on a fast train

When your lover has gone away
Don't it make you feel so sad?
And you go on a journey way into the land
And you start breaking down
'Cos you're under the strain
And you jump on a fast train

You had to go on the lam you stepped into no-man's land
Ain't nobody here on your waveband
Ain't nobody gonna give you a helping hand
And you start breaking down
And just go into the sound
When you hear that fast train

And you keep moving on to the sound of the wheels
And deep inside your heart you really know oh, just how it
    feels
And you start breaking down and go into the pain
Keep on moving on a fast train

You're way over the line
Next thing you're out of your mind
And you're out of your depth
In through the window she crept

Oh there's nowhere to go in the sleet and the snow
Just keep on moving on a fast train

You had to go on the lam stepping in no-man's land
Ain't nobody here on your waveband
Nobody even gonna lend you a helping hand
Oh and you're so alone, can you really make it on your own
Keep on moving on a fast train

Oh going nowhere, except on a fast train
Oh trying to get away from the past
Oh keep on moving keep on moving on a fast train
Going nowhere, across the desert sand, through the barren
   waste
On a fast train going nowhere
On a fast train going nowhere

Whinin' Boy Moan

Drop that coin right into the slot
Get it whether you're ready or not
Let the whinin' boy moan
Let the whinin' boy moan
Let the whinin' boy moan
If you don't know how to do it yourself

Well they call him Mr Jellyroll
It's just the way he rolls his dough
Let the whinin' boy moan
Let the whinin' boy moan
Let the whinin' boy moan
If you don't know how to do it yourself

Well let the whinin' boy moan
If you don't know how to do it yourself
Let the whinin' boy moan
If you don't know how to do it yourself
'Cos he can do it better, better than anyone else
Whine, whine, whine, whine

All the winos down on Market Street
Roll on over to old North Beach
Let the whinin' boy moan
Let the whinin' boy moan
Let the whinin' boy moan
If you don't know how to do it yourself

Well he gonna sing and play for you
Exactly what he's s'pposed to do
Let the whinin' boy moan

Let the whinin' boy moan
Let the whinin' boy moan
If you don't know how to do it yourself
Whine, whine, whine

Let the whinin' boy moan
If you don't know how to do it yourself
Let the whinin' boy moan
If you don't know how to do it yourself
'Cos he can do it better, better than anyone else

Too Many Myths

Too many myths
People just assuming things that aren't true
There's too many myths
Coming between me and you
You might have your name up in lights
But you still have to keep your game uptight

Too many myths
Tell me, tell me how you gonna cope with this
Too many myths
You act like you've never been kissed
You put your name up in lights
And now you gotta keep your game uptight

You got problems
I got problems too
Everybody's gonna think
There must be something wrong with you because

There's just too many myths
Can't you see I'm just trying to stay in the game?
Just too many myths
I'm just trying to maintain
Sure I got my name in lights
But I've still gotta keep my game uptight

You got problems
And I got problems too
But that doesn't necessarily mean that
There's something wrong with you

There's just too many myths
Baby I'm just trying to stay in the game
There's far too many myths
I'm just trying to maintain
I got my name up in lights
But I'm just trying to keep my game uptight

Goldfish Bowl

What will it take for them to leave me alone
Don't they know I'm just a guy who sings songs
I'm not promoting no hit record
And I don't have no TV show
And I don't have no reason to live in the goldfish bowl

I'm just doing my gigs
And I'm on and off the road
Everything I say is not meant to be set in stone
Just because they call me a celebrity
That does not make it true
'Cos I don't believe in the myth people
So why should you

Jazz, Blues & Funk
That's not Rock & Roll
Folk with a beat
And a little bit of Soul
I don't have no hit record
I don't have no TV show
Tell me why should I have to live in this goldfish bowl

Well there's parasites and psychic vampires
Feeding on the public at large
Projecting their shadow onto everyone else
Well the newspaper barons
Are scum of the lowest degree
And they prey on everybody
They prey on you and me

I'm singing Jazz, Blues & Funk

Baby that's not Rock & Roll
Folk with a beat
And a little bit of Soul
I don't have no hit record
I don't have no TV show
So why should I want to live in this goldfish bowl

So why should I have to live in this goldfish bowl?

Little Village

Little village baby, ain't large enough to be a town
From the little village baby, ain't large enough to be a town
Gotta get away from the city
It's gonna bring you down

Heard the voice of the silence, in the evening
In the long cool summer nights
Heard the voice of the silence, in the evening
In the long cool summer night
Telling me not to worry
Everything's gonna be all right

There's only two kinds of truth
Baby let's get it straight from the start
There's only two kinds of truth
Let's get it straight from the start
It's just what you believe
Baby in your head and your heart

Heard the bells ringing
Voices singing soft and low
Heard the bells ringing
Voices were singing soft and low
Way up in the mountain, little village in the snow

Raining in the forest
Just enough to magnetize the leaves
Raining in the forest
Just enough to magnetize the leaves
We'll go walking baby with the moonlight shining down
    through the trees

Little village, way up on the mountainside
Little village baby, way up on the mountainside
Way across the ocean with you by my side

Once in a Blue Moon

Once in a blue moon
Something good comes along
Once in a blue moon
Everything's not going wrong
When you get weary
Beating on the same old gong
Once in a blue moon
Someone like you comes along

Once every once in a while
Something comes along that feels just right
Once every once in a while
Just like switching on an electric light
And sometimes you try till you're blue in the face
But when you get that feeling
Nothing's going to take its place

Once in a blue moon
There's a thing called happiness
It happens when you're in
A state of natural grace

When the wind is blowing
All around the fence
I get that happy feeling
Things start making sense
And you feel so lucky
That you just can't go wrong
Once in a blue moon
Someone like you comes along

Get on with the Show

I just can't seem to take much more of this
Got too much hassle baby and not enough bliss
Got to give these hangers on a miss
'Cos I need some help I just don't get

No one seems to understand what's up
What's up, what's up
So called friends come and go
And things just don't add up
Trying to make my way
Through all this illusion and myth
I don't even have no safety net

Nero fiddled while Rome burnt
Napoleon met his Waterloo
Samson went spare when Delilah cut his hair
But little David slew Goliath too

I'm just trying to get some results
Listen baby I'm not trying to start my own cult
Please tell me something that I don't know
I just wanna get on with the show

Nero fiddled while Rome burnt
Napoleon met his Waterloo
Samson went spare when Delilah cut his hair
But little David slew Goliath too

You'd think some program might do the trick
Let me tell you this wall of fog
Is just too thick

I thought of everything but the whip
But baby nobody on my ship is up to it

I'm just trying to get some results, some results
I'm not trying to start my own cult, no
Just tell me something I don't know
I just wanna get on with the show

I just wanna get on with the show
Just tell me something that I don't know
I just wanna get on with the show
And if it don't work then let it go

Fame

Oh fame, they've taken everything and twisted it
Oh fame they say
You never could have resisted it
What's in a name?
When everybody's jaded by fame

Oh fame again
The press has gone and made another mess of it
Oh just because they've got
So much invested in it
But they say you're to blame it's your own fault
'Cos you got mixed up in fame

Oh no don't believe all that old Andy Warhol guff
It takes a lot more than 10 or 15 minutes
That's just not enough
To qualify you for fame

You went beyond the boundaries of sanity
And every day you defy
All the laws of gravity
You ain't got no shame
'Cos you're just addicted to fame

Oh no don't you buy none of that old Andy Warhol stuff
It takes a lot more than 10 or 15 minutes
That's just not enough
To qualify you for fame

They're already setting up your own Watergate
Oh fame, that stalker out there is just filled with hate

You'll never be the same
'Cos everyone's corrupted by fame

Oh fame, you took away all my humanity
Oh fame got to fight
Every second of the day for my dignity
It's a spectator's game
And there ain't nothin' fair about fame

Oh fame
Oh fame say it again
Oh fame say it again
Fame
They say you're to blame
'Cos you got mixed up in fame

Celtic New Year

If I don't see you through the week
See you through the window
See you next time that we're talking on the telephone
And if I don't see you in that Indian summer
Then I want to see you further on up the road

I said, oh won't you come back?
Have to see you my dear
Won't you come back in the Celtic New Year?
In the Celtic New Year

If I don't see you when I'm going down Louisiana
If I don't see you when I'm down on Bourbon Street
If you don't see me when I'm singing 'Jack O' Diamonds'
If you don't see me when I'm on my lucky streak

Oh, I want you, want you to come on back
I've made it very clear
I want you to come back home in the Celtic New Year
Celtic New Year

If I don't see you when the bonfires are burning, burning
If I don't see you when we're singing the Gloriana tune
If I've got to see you when it's raining deep inside the forest
I got to see you at the waning of the moon

Said oh, won't you come on back?
Want you to be of good cheer
Come back home on the Celtic New Year

Celtic New Year, Celtic New Year

Celtic New Year
In the Celtic New Year
In the Celtic New Year

Come on home, come on home
Come on home, come on home
In the Celtic New Year
In the Celtic New Year

Magic Time

Don't lose the wonder in your eyes
I can see it right now when you smile
Let me go back, for a while
Let me go back, for a while
To that magic time

You can call it nostalgia, I don't mind
Standing on that windswept hillside
Listenin' to the church bells chime
Listen to the church bells chime
In that magic time

Oh the road it never ends
Good to see you my old friend
Once again we sit right down and share the wine

Shivers up and down my spine
It's a feeling so divine
Let me go back for a while
Got to go back for a while
To that magic time

Oh the road it never ends
Good to see you my old friend
Once again we'll sit down and share the wine

Got to go back
And we'll go back in your prime
The sun is gonna shine
When we go back for a while
When we go back for a while

To that magic time

Don't lose the wonder in your eyes
It's right there when you smile
Got to go back, for a while
Got to go back, for a while
To that magic time

Call it nostalgia, I don't mind
Standing on that windswept hillside
Listenin' to the church bells chime
Listenin' to the church bells chime
In that magic time

If we go back, for a while
Let me go back, for a while
To that magic time

Blue and Green

Blue and green
Well my song is blue and green
Blue and green
Well my song is blue and green
What I say
Baby, baby what I mean

Blue up in the sky
And Mother Nature's green
Don't have to wonder why
Just taking in this country scene
Driving through the land
Understanding blue and green

Sometimes it feels like baby
That I've been seeing red
Sometimes it feels like baby
That I've been seeing red
Woke up early one morning
Mr Blue and Green was standing round my bed

Blue and green
That's the colours that I see
Blue, blue, blue, blue, blue and green
But that doesn't mean that you should envy me
Hear what I say, I say what I mean
Oh blue and green

Early in the morning
Sometimes I feel I'm seeing red
Early in the morning

Well I feel I'm seeing red
Gotta blues all in my breakfast
And green all in my head

Blue blue blue blue blue blue blue blue
Blue and green
Sky is blue
And Mother Nature's green
Keep on driving through the land
Taking in the country scene

Behind the Ritual

Drinking wine in the alley, drinking wine in the alley
Making time, drinking that wine
Out of my mind in the days gone by

Making time with Sally, drinking that wine
In the days gone by, talking all out of my mind
Drinking that wine, talking all out of my mind

Spin and turning in the alley, spin and turning in the alley
Like a Whirling Dervish in the alley, drinking that wine
Drinking wine, making time in the days gone by

Boogie-woogie child in the alley
Drinking that wine, making time, talking all out of my mind
Drinking wine in the days gone by, behind the ritual

Behind the ritual, behind the ritual
In the days gone by, drinking that wine
Making time, drinking that wine way back in time

Spin and turn and rhyme in the alley
Spin and turning, making it rhyme, talking all out of my
    mind
Talking that jive, drinking that wine in the days gone by

Drinking wine in the alley, drinking that wine
Making time, talking all out of my mind
Drinking that wine making time in the alley

Behind the ritual, behind the ritual
You find the spiritual, you find the spiritual

Behind the ritual in the days gone by
Drinking wine in the alley, drinking wine in the alley
Making time, talking all out of my mind
Drinking that wine in the days gone by, days gone by

Spin and turn talking that jive
Spin and turn talking that jive all out of our minds
Drinking that sweet wine
Making time, making time in the days gone by

Behind the ritual, behind the ritual
Behind the ritual, behind the ritual
Drinking that wine making time in the days gone by

Behind the ritual, making time in the days gone by

In the days gone by, in the days gone by
Drink that wine, making time
Getting high in the days gone by, drinking that wine

Getting high behind the ritual
Getting high behind the ritual
Drinking that wine in the days gone by

Behind the ritual, behind the ritual
Behind the ritual, behind that spiritual
In the days gone by drinking that wine and getting high

So high behind the ritual, so high behind the ritual
So high in the days gone by
Drinking that wine making time, making time

Stretching time, stretching time
Drinking that wine, stretching time
Stretching time in the days gone by behind the ritual

Behind the ritual
Behind the ritual

How Can a Poor Boy?

Had my congregation, had my flock
When I was a shepherd of men
Chased the wild goose, chased the pot of gold
Chased the rainbows end

How can a poor boy deliver this message to you?
How can a poor boy? You don't believe anything that's true

Had my rise, had my downfall
Now I'm gonna rise up again
Had my degrees, my initiations
Not speaking to the profane

How can a poor boy get this message to you?
How can a poor boy when you don't believe a thing that's
    true?

I've been anointed, been appointed
Even been magnified
Spied a chapel all of gold
The priest was laying down with the swine

How can a poor boy get a little message to you?
How can a poor boy when you don't believe anything is
    true?
How can a poor boy get this message through to you?
How can a poor boy when you don't believe a single thing is
    true?

Watch the illusion of false security
Play of the shadows that move

Tell me what evil lurks in the hearts of men
Only the shadow knows

How can a poor boy get this message to you?
How can a poor boy when you don't believe a thing that's
    true, for you
When you don't believe a thing, nothing that's true for you
How can a poor boy ever get next to you?

Open the Door (to Your Heart)

Open the door to your heart
Open the door to your soul
Get back in the flow
Open the door to your heart

Money doesn't make you fulfilled
Money's just to pay the bills
It's need not greed
Open the door to your heart

You've got eyes to see
And ears to hear
Then why don't you quit
Crying in your beer my dear

If nobody gets what they want
Tell me what's the use in that
Everybody just gets fat
Open the door to your heart

Backbiters always make mistakes
If you want to get an even break
Think of everything that's at stake
Open the door to your heart

Don't you think I know who my enemies are?
Their slip is showing and the door is ajar
Well this time they pushed me too far
Open the door to your heart

If you've got eyes to see

And ears to hear
You better quit, quit
Crying in your beer my dear

If you can't hear the song you're wrong
I've been around too long
Just listen to the words that's all
Open the door to your heart
Open the door to your heart
Open the door to your soul
Got to get back in the flow
Open the door to your heart

Come on
Open the door to your heart
Open the door to your soul
Get back in the flow
Open the door to your heart

Come on, come on, come on
Come on, come on, come on

Open the door to your heart
Open the door to your soul
Got to get back in the flow now
Open the door to your heart

Come on, come on, come on,
Come on, come on, come on

Open the door to your heart

Goin' Down to Monte Carlo

Goin' down to Monte Carlo about 25K from Nice
Goin' down to Monte Carlo about 25K from Nice
Got to get myself together, gotta get my head some peace

Sartre said that hell is other people, I believe that most of
    them are
Sartre said hell is other people, I believe that most of them
    are
Well their pettiness amazes me, even after I'm gone this far

Goin' down to Monte Carlo 25K from Nice
Goin' down to Monte Carlo 'bout 25K from Nice
Gotta get my head together, gotta get my head some peace.

Playing in the background some kind of phoney pseudo jazz
Playing in the background in the restaurant, some kind of
    phoney pseudo jazz
I don't care I'm trying to get away from people, that are
    trying to drive me mad

After everything I've worked for, not goin' to throw
    everything away
After everything I worked so hard for, I'm not goin' to give it
    all away
I just need to take a rain check, I can live to fight another day

Goin' down to Monte Carlo, 25K from Nice
Goin' down, goin' down to Monte Carlo, still about 25K
    from Nice
Got to get my head showered, got to find some release

Born to Sing

Man can be king
Seems to have everything
But it comes with a sting
When you were born to sing

Reason doesn't walk in
It's not done on a whim
Passion's everything
When you were born to sing

Feeling good
Singing the blues
It ain't easy
Keep on paying dues

When it gets to the part
Well let's not stop and start
Deep down in your heart
You know you were born to sing

When you came in
No original sin
You were a king
Because you were born to sing

Reason doesn't walk in
It's not done on a whim
Passion's everything
When you were born to sing

Lord, feeling good

Singing the blues
Keep on keeping on
Paying them dues

When it comes to the part
Well let's not stop and start
Deep down in your heart
Baby you were born to sing

When it gets to the part
When the band starts to swing
Then you know everything
'Cause you were born to sing

When it gets to the part
When the band starts to swing
Then you know everything
'Cause you were born to sing

Close Enough for Jazz

No use feeling sad
No use staying mad
Better when you're glad
You can be there in a heartbeat
When it's close enough for jazz
Close enough for jazz

Be glad with what you have
Even if it's half
Empty in the glass
If there's room to move your elbows
Then it's close enough for jazz
Close enough for jazz

When you're not in a hurry
When things may turn around
Never give in to worry
Try looking up not down, don't frown

Close enough for jazz
Is it Persil is it Daz?
Well it doesn't really matter
When it's better on the inside
And it's close enough for jazz
Close enough for jazz
Close enough for jazz
Close enough for jazz

Retreat and View

From my retreat and view
Make my own break through
And I might see things new
From my retreat and view

There's visions to behold
Treasures to unfold
Home away from home
From my retreat and view

Well the higher you go
The more that you know you can find
Like a memory that's there
Stuck in the back of your mind

There's bargains of the soul
Dreams that do unfold
Now I know it's true
From my retreat and view

There's bargains of the soul
Treasures to behold
Some time to start anew
From my retreat and view

From my retreat and view
Got to make my own break through
So I can see things new
From my retreat and view

High up on the mountainside

From my retreat and view
The place to satisfy
From my retreat and view

From my retreat and view
Got to make my own break through
So I can see things new
From my retreat and view

Pagan Heart

My pagan heart
My pagan soul
Got to move on to the crossroads
Got to go to the arcadian groves
Got to move to the crossroads
Down by the crossroads, crossroads

My pagan heart
My pagan soul
Got to go to the holy wood
When the sun is good, to the holy wood
You take it in, it's under your skin
It tastes like wine
In the evening time
Down by the crossroads
Down by the crossroads

My pagan heart
My pagan soul
Down, down, down, down
Down by the arcadian groves
Down, down, down, down,
Down by arcadian groves
By the roads
By the roads
My pagan heart
My pagan soul

My pagan heart
My pagan soul
I got to go down, by the crossroads

The moon is rising
In the evening time
By the crossroads, crossroads
My pagan heart
My pagan soul

Down down down down
Down by the arcadian grove
Down down down down
Down by the arcadian grove
Got to go down by the crossroads, crossroads
My pagan heart
My pagan soul
My pagan heart
My pagan soul
Got to go down by the crossroads, crossroads
Pagan heart
My pagan soul
Got to go down
To the crossroads

I look at the sun, I take it in
It's under my skin
Pagan heart
Pagan soul
Pagan heart
Pagan soul
I've got to know
I got to know
Pagan heart
Pagan soul
Put a spell on you
Put a spell on you
Down by the crossroads
My pagan heart

My pagan soul
Pagan heart
Pagan soul
Put a spell on you
Down by the crossroads
When the moon was new
When the moon was new
Put a spell on you

In Tiburon

Across the bay the fog is lifting
And I am here in Tiburon
That's what she said
When she was sitting looking out at the Golden Gate
In the morning dawn

Across the bay in San Francisco
Where City Lights and Ferlinghetti stay
North Beach alleyways and cafes
Kerouac and Ginsberg
Gregory Corso and Neal Cassady all held sway

Vince Guaraldi would play 'Cast Your Fate to the Wind' in
    the distance
Lenny Bruce got busted at 'The Hungry Eye'
The 'No-Name Bar' down in Sausalito
Across the street where Chet Baker used to play

My heart was beating on the hillside
Near Belvedere and Tiburon
I need to take you back, back down to 'Frisco
Now we need each other, need each other to lean on

Vince Guaraldi would play 'Cast Your Fate to the Wind'
and we'd listen
In the evening across the way
Chet Baker would play down at the Trident
With his horn he blew everybody away

The Cliff House down at the Sea Rock Hotel
Foghorns blowing all night long till dawn

Geary Street culchies left their homeland a long while ago
Some have stayed, but others not for so long

My heart was beating on the hillside
Near Belvedere and Tiburon
Take you back down to San Francisco
Now we need each other more than ever to lean on
Now we need each other more than ever, more than ever to
    lean on

Lean on me
Lean on
Now we need each other more than ever to lean on

Back to City Lights, City Lights
North Beach and Broadway
We need each other

We need each other to lean on

Back to City Lights and North Beach
North Beach and Broadway
We need each other, need each other to lean on

Across the bay in Tiburon
Across the bay in Tiburon
And across the bay in Tiburon
And across the bay in Tiburon

Look Beyond the Hill

When your troubles are a burden let your mind be still
Wait until the clouds start moving way beyond the hill

Can't you see the sky is bluer up upon the ridge
Just don't let the green grass fool you, look beyond the hill

Sometime it don't rhyme, seem to have your fill
Got to get your house in order in line with your will

Tomorrow is another day to go in for the kill
You can have a change of heart now
Look beyond the hill

You got to look beyond the hill
You got to look beyond the hill

Memory Lane

It's autumn time, going on November
I view the leaves in all their splendour
Is it déjà vu, I just can't remember
I stop a while and take in the scene

I stop a while and ask a stranger
Is this the place that was once called Memory Lane?
I don't know where I am or what I'm after
I'm stuck here again back on Memory Lane

Now the leaves are falling and it's coming on to winter
Nights keep getting shorter and shorter every day
One sign up ahead says 'danger'
Another one says 'stop'
One says 'yield this way'

And it swerves and moves around the corners
And there's flashing lights up ahead 'round the bend
Road curves and twists and turns and twists and turns and
    wanders
'Til you get, 'til you get to the very end

Now I'm back here again with more questions than answers
And I'm standing in the pouring rain
There's something moving, moving in the shadows
And it's getting dark now up on Memory Lane

I stop a while and ask some strangers
Is this the place that was once called Memory Lane?
I don't know where I am, don't know what I'm after
I'm stuck here back up on Memory Lane

I stop a while and ask some strangers
Is this the place that once was called Memory Lane?
Don't know where I am right now or what I'm after
I'm stuck here up, stuck on Memory Lane
I'm stuck here up, back on Memory Lane
I'm stuck here back up on Memory Lane
I'm stuck here back, back up on Memory Lane

The Pen Is Mightier than the Sword

You've got to live by the pen 'cause it's mightier than the
    sword
You've got to live by the pen 'cause it's mightier than the
    sword
Every man is me every man is you
I can't tell you what you've got to do
You've got to live by the pen, it's mightier than the sword

You've got to live by the pen 'cause it's mightier than the
    sword
You've got to live by the pen 'cause it's mightier than the law
Every man is me every man is you
I can't tell you what you have to do
You've got to live by the pen 'cause it's mightier than the
    sword

You've got to live by the pen 'cause it's mightier than the law
You've got to live by the pen 'cause of what you saw
Every man is me every man is you
I can't tell you what you're supposed to do
I've got to live by the pen 'cause it's mightier than the sword

I've got to live by the pen 'cause it's mightier than the sword
I've got to live by the pen 'cause it's mightier than the sword
Every man is me every man is you
But I can't tell you what you have to do
I've got to live by the pen 'cause it's mightier than the sword

They're gonna get burned 'cause they're playing with fire
They're gonna get caught 'cause somebody is a liar
Every man is me every man is you

I can't tell you what you're supposed to do
You've got to live by the pen 'cause it's mightier than the
    sword

I've got to live by the pen 'cause it's mightier than the sword
I've got to live by the pen 'cause it's mightier than the sword
Every man is me every man is you
I can't tell you what you're supposed to do
I've got to live by my pen 'cause it's mightier than the law
I've got to live by my pen 'cause it's mightier than the sword
I've got to live by my pen 'cause it's mightier than the sword

Transformation

Gonna be a transformation in your heart and soul
Gonna be a transformation baby now that you know
Get used to righteousness when it makes you feel whole
Gonna be a transformation baby down in your soul

Remember when we were downhearted didn't have nowhere
    to go
And the wisdom of insecurity just knowing that we know
Then something starts happening feel like you're on a roll
Gonna be a transformation baby down in your soul

God's like a river keeps on wanting to flow
Keeps on advancing with the wisdom you know
Time has a rhythm when the love is the law
Love is forever baby down in your soul

Gonna be a transformation baby down in your soul
Gonna be a transformation now that you know
Get used to righteousness 'cause it makes you feel whole

Gonna be a transformation down in your soul
Gonna be a transformation down in your soul
Gonna be a transformation baby now that you know

Get used to righteousness 'cause it makes you feel whole
Gonna be a transformation right down in your soul

Gonna be a transformation, down in your soul
Gonna be a transformation, down in your soul

Broken Record

Baby, stall the gate for me
Take me, lift me out of my misery
Lift my spirit up, and set me free

When things are driving me insane
Let me hear that same refrain
Over and over and over
And over and over and over and over again

Take it to the break
Don't make any mistake
For goodness sake
Have to stay awake

Broken record, broken record, broken record
Broken record, broken record, broken record
Broken record, broken record, broken record
Broken record, broken record, broken record
Broken record, broken record

Take it to the break
Make no mistake
Stay awake
Whatever it takes

Broken record, broken record, broken record
Broken record, broken record, broken record
Broken record, broken record, broken record
Broken record, broken record, broken record
Broken record, broken record, broken record

Broken record, broken record, broken record
Broken record, broken record, broken record
Broken record, broken record, broken record
Broken record, broken record, broken record
Broken record, broken record

5am Greenwich Mean Time

Well I'm thinking about my people and the love that we once
  had
Well I'm thinking about my people and the love that we once
  had
But I don't understand how everything got so bad

Well I'm walking in the morning and I'm talking all to myself
Well I'm walking in the morning and I'm talking all to myself
And it's 5am and its Greenwich Mean Time

Well I'm wondering what happened to my baby child
And I'm wondering what happened to my baby child
Gonna drive me crazy, gonna drive me wild

Well I'm walking in the morning and I'm walking all by
  myself
Well I'm walking in the morning and I'm talking all by myself
Well it's 5am and I think I'm gonna need some help

Well I'm walking up the hillside and I'm trying to catch the
  bus on time
Well I'm walking up the hillside and I'm trying to catch my
  bus on time
You see you do anything to keep everybody satisfied

And I'm wondering what happened to my baby child
And I'm wondering what happened to my baby child
I'm walking in the morning and it's 5am Greenwich Mean
  Time

Yeah, thinking about my people and the love that we once had

Well I'm thinking about my people and the love that we once
   had
Well I don't understand how everything just got so bad

I'm walking in the morning and I'm talking all by myself
Well I'm walking in the morning and I'm talking all by myself
It's 5am and I think I'm gonna need some help

I'm walking in the morning, Greenwich Mean Time
I'm walking in the morning, Greenwich Mean Time
It's 5am and I think I'm gonna lose my mind

Well I'm walking in the morning and it's 5am Greenwich
   Mean Time

Ain't Gonna Moan No More

Oh oh oh ain't gonna moan no more
Oh oh oh ain't gonna moan no more
Ain't no wolf at my door
Ain't gonna moan no more

From the Old Groaner to the deep deep blues
Muddy Waters and John Lee too
From the master of vocalese
Jon Hendricks sang it with ease
Ain't gonna moan no more

Satchmo chose playin' the clown
It didn't stop him layin' it down
He chose to smile instead of frown
He kept playin' his gigs and movin' from town to town

No time to frown
Ain't gonna moan today
Goin' to town gonna make my day
Do my best to create all the better space
Ain't gonna moan no more, man
Around this place

Willie The Shake said that 'life is what you make it'
Somebody else said, 'fake it till you make it'
Well I feel much better when my feet are touchin' the ground
I get hip to the tip when I hear that lonesome sound

Some people's down
Someone else is upbeat
Transform the norm, tryin' to make it sweet

When you know things are happening
Well it just can't be beat
When you know the score
You don't have to moan no more

Oh oh oh ain't gonna moan no more
Oh woah ain't gonna moan no more
Ain't no wolf at my door
Ain't gonna moan no more

Oh oh oh

Ain't no wolf at my door
Ain't gonna moan no more
Oh oh oh hey, ain't gonna moan no more
Oh oh oh ain't gonna moan no more
When you know the score
Don't have to moan no more

Love Is Hard Work

Love is hard work that's a fact
Think you're moving forward but it's setback after setback
Love is hard work that's an actual fact
Think you're moving forward but it's setback after setback

No such thing as standard no such thing as norm
Think you know it then your sanity is gone
Love is hard work baby, that's a fact
Think you're moving forward but it's setback after setback

Some people say love's a mugs' game
Feel like leaving on the midnight train
Trying to play your part what stage does it become fun?
Love is hard work now it's got me on the run

Love is hard work baby that's a fact
Two steps forward and three steps back
Love is hard work now now, man that's a fact
Think you're moving but it's setback after setback

Love is hard work baby, that's a fact
Two steps forward and three steps back
Love is hard work, that's an actual fact
When you think you're moving it's setback after setback

Some people say love's a mugs' game
Feel like leaving on the midnight train
But I've got to double back, double back
Love is hard work now baby, that's a fact

Love is hard work, love is hard work

Love is hard work, baby that's a fact
When you think you're moving it's setback after setback

Spirit Will Provide

Spirit will provide beyond the lie
Spirit will provide beyond the why
Spirit will provide, spirit will provide

Let go, let go then spirit will provide
Change your thought and it will change your mind
Spirit will provide, spirit will provide

It's no mystery when you can see clearly
Vibrating at a higher frequency
Fill your purpose as you go about life daily
Understanding what it means to clearly see

Spirit will provide when you feel down
Plug into don't buy what's goin' round
Spirit will provide, spirit will provide

It's no mystery when you can see clearly
Vibrating, vibrating at the higher frequency
Fulfilling your purpose as you go about life daily
Understanding what it means to clearly see

Spirit will provide now dry your eyes
Spirit will provide now don't you cry
Spirit will provide, spirit will provide
Spirit will provide, spirit will provide

Spirit will provide, spirit will provide
Spirit will provide, spirit will provide

The Prophet Speaks

When the prophet speaks
Mostly no one listens
When the prophet speaks and no one hears
Only those who have ears to listen
Only those who are trained to hear

Come closer now
I'll tell you with a whisper
Close and I will whisper it in your ear
What big ears you've got when you get the details
Do you understand
Do I make it clear

When the prophet speaks
And no one listens
When the prophet speaks
Mostly no one hears
Only those that are trained to listen
Only those who have ears to hear

When the prophet speaks and no one listens
Baby, don't you have no fear
You gotta get the truth of what is happening
When the prophet speaks, have to make it clear
Come closer now, and I will whisper
Whisper the secret in your ear
What big ears you've got when you get all the details
Do you understand, do I make myself clear

When the prophet speaks you've gotta listen
When the prophet speaks you've got to get the truth

When the prophet speaks don't need no explanation
When the prophet speaks, have to make it move

Prophet speaks no one listens
When the prophet speaks mainly nobody hears
Only those that are trained to listen
Only those who have ears to hear

Acknowledgements

Special thanks to Eamonn Hughes for his assistance with editing this second volume and for once again shining a light on the narrative flowing through the titles. Sincere thanks to Paul Muldoon for his insight. Thanks also to Kerry, Sarah and Kate on the Exile team.

Lyrics credits

Index of Titles and First lines

Song titles are in italic; first lines are in roman